Clarke, James Freeman
Anti-slavery days

**DATE DUE**

| | | | |
|---|---|---|---|
| MAY 1 0 '72 | | | |
| NOV 15 '72 | | | |
| JUL 18 '73 | | | |
| NOV 20 '74 | | | |
| DEC 3 '7? | | | |
| JUN 15 77 | | | |
| NOV 15 '7? | | | |
| NOV 28 ?4 | | | |
| | | | |
| | | | |
| | | | |

# ANTI-SLAVERY DAYS.

## A SKETCH OF THE STRUGGLE WHICH ENDED IN THE ABOLITION OF SLAVERY IN THE UNITED STATES.

By JAMES FREEMAN CLARKE.

Is true freedom but to break
Fetters for our own dear sake,
And, with leathern hearts, forget
That we owe mankind a debt?
No ! true freedom is to share
All the chains our brothers wear,
And, with heart and hand, to be
Earnest to make others free
                    LOWELL.

**NEGRO UNIVERSITIES PRESS**
WESTPORT, CONNECTICUT

Originally published in 1883
by J. W. Lovell Company, New York

Reprinted 1970 by
Negro Universities Press
A Division of Greenwood Press, Inc.
Westport, Conn.


SBN 8371-3286-X

# DEDICATION.

-------

## TO THE MEMORY OF

# ELLIS GRAY LORING

### AND

# LOUISA LORING;

THE WISE, GENEROUS AND TRUE FRIENDS OF EVERY GOOD

CAUSE,

THESE CHAPTERS ARE DEDICATED.

# TABLE OF CONTENTS.

## CHAPTER I.

### THE ORIGIN OF THE ANTI-SLAVERY MOVEMENTS IN THE UNITED STATES.

## CHAPTER II.

### THE FIGHT IN CONGRESS.

## CHAPTER V.

### ANTI-SLAVERY IN POLITICS.

## CHAPTER VI.

### THE COMBAT DEEPENS.

## CHAPTER VII.

### CIVIL WAR AND END OF SLAVERY.

# INTRODUCTION.

THE following brief sketch of the conflict which led to the emancipation of four millions of slaves in the United States, is intended chiefly for the generation which has grown up since those stirring scenes. They are, naturally, for the most part, little acquainted with it. Recent history is that of which people know the least, with the exception of those who have taken part in it. Children are taught in the schools about the battle of Marathon, but not about the battle of Gettysburg. They learn in the Sunday-Schools all about the emancipation of the Hebrews from Egyptian slavery, but very little about that of the colored people in the United States. Yet this story, when it comes to be fitly told, will be found as intensely interesting as any series of events in the records of mankind. I do not hope to do more in these chapters (originally given as lectures) than to call attention to a few important events and characters belonging to the period described.

The hot passions of that time have now grown cool. The people engaged in that conflict can understand each other better. We, of the North, can see more clearly the difficulties under which the slave-owners labored. Slavery spread like an iron network over their society—it was connected with all their habits and interests. They did not see how it was possible to emancipate their slaves without rending asunder the whole fabric of their society. And if they did not decide to plunge into the unknown dangers and terrors of emancipation, they were compelled, by an inexorable logic, to bind the chains of their slaves tighter day by day, and to resist, by every possible means, everything which disturbed their perfect submission and entire docility. The aggressions of the slave-power, which finally drove the North into the anti-slavery movement, seemed to the slaveholders necessary measures of defence. In their determination not to yield, they seized every weapon which came in their way. Their determined and compact purpose gained them so many successes, that at last they took the fatal leap which ended in the destruction of the whole evil system, and the coming of a better day.

And now the South and the North are both agreed that emancipation was the greatest of blessings. Now a new prosperity, solid and increasing, has taken the place of the old in all the Southern States. Now

the North and South are really one, as they never
were before the war. Now we have a common country, united interests, the same ends. Now we can af-
ford to retrace that period of tempestuous struggle,
endeavoring to do justice to both contending parties.
Now we have in reality, and not in mere words,
" Union and Freedom, now and forever, one and in-
separable." The terrible war came like the thunder
storm, purifying the air, and leaving such a blessing
behind it as no war before ever did, enabling us to
use sincerely the great words of Lowell :—

> O beautiful ! My country ! Ours once more !
> Smoothing thy gold of war-dishevelled hair
> O'er such sweet brows as never other wore,—
> And letting thy set lips,
> Freed from war's pale eclipse,
> The rosy edges of their smile lay bare .
> What were our lives without thee ?
> What all our lives to save thee?
> We reck not what we gave thee ;
> We do not dare to doubt thee.
> But ask whatever else and we will dare.

In these imperfect narrations I have naturally
dwelt mostly on the events with which I was per-
sonally familiar, and the persons with whom I happened to be best acquainted. I have therefore confined my relation within narrower limits than would
be proper in anything claiming to be a history. The
scenes of the drama which I describe are chiefly laid
in Massachusetts, and the characters are New England men. I have given the view taken by this class

of actors, and have only hinted at the way in which men felt and thought in other sections of the country. This little work is, therefore, only one contribution to the future history of those days—one of the "Memoires pour servir" for the more complete work which is to be written hereafter.

# ANTI-SLAVERY DAYS.

## CHAPTER I.

### ORIGIN OF ANTI-SLAVERY IN THE UNITED STATES.

> " If we have whispered truth,
>   Whisper no longer;
> Speak as the trumpet does,
>   Sterner and stronger."
>                         —WHITTIER.

I propose in this work to give a brief sketch of the greatest moral conflict of modern times. We shall see how an immense institution, fortified by law, solidly bound together by pecuniary interests, upheld by political combinations, sustained by custom, fashion, prejudice, and the fear of change, was attacked by a few men whose only weapon was a perpetual appeal to the human reason, the human conscience, and the human heart. We shall see in what way this attack was resisted ; how the institution gathered more and more power ; gained the alliance of the two great political parties : annexed vast territories and opened them to slavery ; took

possession of Congress, the Presidency, the Supreme
Court of the United States, and by a series of Acts
of Congress seemed to have entrenched itself against
all assaults, and become stronger than ever before
We shall see how, while this political power was passing into the hands of slaveholders, the moral power
of the country was steadily accumulating in those of
their opponents, until at last the war of tongue and
pen changed into the greatest military struggle of
modern times  We shall hear the first Southern gun
fired at Fort Sumter, and see the people of the North
uniting as one man to put down the rebellion ; vast
armies springing as if born out of the earth ; great navies
organized to blockade the long coast line of the South ;
and shall glance at some events in the terrible war of
four years, from the bombardment of Sumter, April
12th, 1861, to the surrender of Lee, April 9th, 1865.
We shall see how slavery went down in that dreadful
conflict, never to rise again—how, in a single generation, and in the lifetime of the chief agitator himself,
this vast revolution was accomplished.   Never in
human history has there been such an example of
the power of conscience in gaining a victory over
worldly interest ; and it ought to be an encouragement forever, for all who contend for lowly right
against triumphant wrong, for unpopular truth against
fashion, prejudice and power.

   It is nearly eighteen years since these events came

to an end. The passions of men have cooled, a new South has sprung from the ruins of the old, another generation has come upon the stage. The North and South are truly one; the American Union, this single root of bitterness having been taken away, is vastly more powerful, and more united, than ever. We can now speak I trust, without prejudice or severity of those who differed from us or from whom we differed. Though we may still think they were wrong, we can see how their conduct may have seemed to them right, or, at least, how it was natural for them to think so, under their circumstances.

The seeds of freedom and of slavery were planted in this country in the same year. In 1620 the May Flower brought the Pilgrim Fathers to Plymouth; in 1620 a Dutch ship entered James River in Virginia with twenty African slaves. One of these ships brought free institutions to our shores; the other brought slavery. From that time until the beginning of the American Revolution the whole power of England supported and encouraged the African slave trade. Under that encouragement more than 300,-000 African slaves were imported into thirteen British colonies. Alarmed by the rapid increase of slaves, the planters of Virginia, in 1726, levied a tax on their importation, and South Carolina did the same in 1760. The legislature of Pennsylvania in 1712 had passed a similar act. Massachusetts endeavored to abolish the slave trade in 1771 and 1774 by act of legislature. All of these colonial acts were vetoed by the authority of the British crown. The prosperity of England was thought to be involved in maintaining the slave trade ; and the mother country steadily refused all attempts of the colonists to prohibit it. Thus the evil gradually extended itself, and became rooted in the habits of the people, and especially in the Southern States. Love of power, love of money, and love of ease, all were enlisted on its side. And when by discovery of the cotton-gin, Eli Whitney,* made slavery a source of great wealth, it became dangerous to speak against it in the cotton-growing states.

There were however, always those who saw and proclaimed the sin and evil of holding a man as a slave. By the laws of slavery, in this country, a man was turned into a thing ; he had no rights ; he could be bought and sold like a horse or an ox ; he could be torn from his wife and children, or they could be taken from him whenever the owner pleased. In the hands of a cruel master, he could be beaten to death, or burned alive, and no power could prevent it. He might have so little negro blood as to pass for a white man, but as long as his mother was a slave, he was a slave too. Young girls, even those almost white might be sold at their master's will to any one who wished to buy them ; and they had no safety, no pro-

*Aided in this invention by the widow of Gen. Greene.

tection.  The possession of absolute power often seems
to make fiends of men, and that most fiendish of all
sins, cruelty, grew and flourished in those whose
power over their slaves was unrestrained by conscience
or religion.

It seemed impossible that any thoughtful person
could believe such an institution as this to be right.
It took from the slave all his rights at one blow—it
left him nothing.   Christianity said, " Do to others as
you would have them  do  to you," and " Love your
neighbor as yourself."   The  declaration of Independence, the organic law of our  Union,  standing above
the Constitution itself, begins—" We hold these truths
to be self-evident, that all men were made equal, and
were endowed by their Creator with inalienable rights,
among which are life, liberty, and the pursuit of happiness."   How reconcile slavery with these great laws
of God and man ?   Very early, therefore, there was
opposition made to slavery—an opposition founded on
moral, religious, social, and political reasons,   The
apostle *John Elliot*, in 1675, presented a memorial
against the slavery of Indians and others to the Colonial  Legislature of Massachusetts.   Judge *Samuel
Sewall*, of Boston, in 1700, printed a pamphlet against
negro slavery.

The body of Quakers early agitated the  question.
Many eminent Friends gave' their  testimony against
slavery.   John Woolman praised by  Charles Lamb.

travelled through the Middle and Southern States between 1746 and 1767, and everywhere told the Friends that the practice of slavery was not right. He said that wherever slavery prevailed " he saw a dark gloominess overhanging the land, and the spirit of fierceness and love of dominion in the people."

Anthony Benezet, the Huguenot ; Elias Hicks, founder of the Hicksite sect of Quakers ; Benjamin Lundy, the teacher of Garrison, uttered their protests against the system, and devoted their lives to pointing out its evils. John Wesley, who saw it in Georgia, called it " the sum of all villanies." Dr. Samuel Hopkins, of Newport R.I., a place which was in his time the very seat of the slave trade, preached, in the year 1770, against that trade, and against the holding of slaves, to a congregation engaged in that business. And there have been few greater examples of heroism in the pulpit than was shown by him on that occasion.

The Constitution of Massachusetts was adopted in 1780, before the end of the revolutionary war, and its Bill of Rights declares that all men are born free and equal. The Supreme Court of Massachusetts, by the voice of Judge Lowell, decided that this declaration abolished slavery in Massachusetts forever. By that decision, all the slaves at that time held in Massachusetts became free. The system had, however, never been oppressive in Massachusetts. It was tempered

by the principles and by the habits of the people.
Slaves in New England, generally, were regarded as
members of the household. They lived with the
family and were treated as belonging to it, and after
they were free they usually continued to live as before, working for the family and being taken care of-
These former slaves were thus provided for until their
death. I, myself, remember seeing, when I was a
boy, some of those old colored men and women in
several families. I recollect an old woman called
Phœbe, who used to sit by the kitchen fire in the
family of my uncle Williams, and there was another,
old Tillo as he was called, in the family of my grandfather Hull. He considered himself always as much
a member of the household as any of the children or
grandchildren.

The first abolition society in this country was
formed in wennsylvania, and Franklin became its
President in 1787. The New York Abolition Society
was founded in 1785. Chief-Justice John Jay was its
first President, and Alexander Hamilton was its Secretary. In 1791, Jonathan Edwards, Jr., declared that
to hold a man as a slave is man-stealing, and a great
sin in the sight of God. We all remember the sentiments of President Jefferson on this Subject. We
know how, in his " Notes on Virginia," he described
the evil effects of slave-holding on the manners and
morals,of the people, and especially on the young, who,

from the very hours of childhood, formed habits of
violent, arbitrary and wilful conduct.   He foresaw
that the time must come in which there would be a
conflict between slavery and freedom, "And in such a
conflict as this," said he " God has no attribute which
can take part with the slaveholders."    " I tremble for
my country when I remember that God is just."

In the year 1787, in the first continental Congress,
there was passed an ordinance, brought forward by
Nathan Dane, of Massachusetts, prohibiting all slavery
north and west of the Ohio.   By this ordinance, Ohio,
Indiana and Illinois were saved from slavery for freedom.   The inhabitants of Indiana, headed by Wm.
H. Harrison, petitioned Congress to be allowed to
have that ordinance suspended for a short time so
that they might have the use of slaves in opening the
country.   Many of them had emigrated from Kentucky
and were accustomed to slavery.   But Congress again
and again refused consent to their petition, and the
slaveholders in Congress—such men as John Ran-
dolph taking the lead—were among the first to declare that it would be a great evil to allow slavery to
invade that territory.

There were formerly two opposing sentiments at
the South on this question.   One party held that
slavery was wrong ; that it was an evil, and that it
must gradually disappear ; that it must by degrees
come to an end.   The other maintained that slavery

was profitable, that it gave power to the South ; that
it prevented the necessity of white labor ; and, therefore, that it must be retained, and, if necessary, extended. Both these sentiments found their way into
the Constitution. To please one party, the words
" slave " and " slavery " are not mentioned in that instrument. For " slaves " we have the euphemism,
" Persons held to labor," and " all other persons."
But the opposite party obtained the advantage of
having three provisions inserted in the Constitution,
the first and most important of which was that three-
fifths of the slaves were to be counted as voters, so
that the slaveowners were allowed to vote not only
for themselves, but also for their property. Many of
the most important successes of the slave-power afterward were owing to that undue advantage which they
obtained by this constitutional provision.

The second advantage gained by the slave-holding
interest was that the importation of slaves was allowed
until the year 1800. Those thus imported, however,
are not called slaves, but " such persons as any of the
States now existing shall think proper to admit."
This was the roundabout way in which it was then
considered decent to speak of slavery.

The third provision in the Constitution for maintaining slavery, was that which provided for the return
of fugitives. This was expressed in a still more obscure way. " No person held to labor or service in

one State under the laws thereof, escaping into another, shall be discharged from such service or labor, but shall be delivered up on claim of the party to whom such labor or service is due." Some thought that if this were construed grammatically, it declared (as John Quincy Adams once pointed out) that no such refugees should be returned. It was, however, well understood that that was by no means the intention of those who drew up the Constitution, and it was never construed according to the rules of strict grammar, but in precisely the opposite way. Many of the Abolitionists claimed that the Constitution was a pro-slavery instrument. Those who belonged to the political anti-slavery parties called it an anti-slavery instrument. To me it seems that both were right. It was a pro-slavery instrument, and also an anti-slavery instrument. It was an inconsistent instrument.

The slaveholders were bound together by the power of a common interest, by the sense of a common danger, and by the superior discipline of will which they developed from their position as masters over people wholly subservient to their will. Down to the time of the civil war they were continually gaining more and more strength and influence in the general government. Although it was computed that there were in the South only some three hundred and fifty or four hundred thousand slaveholders, they nevertheless had the entire control of the Southern States.

They governed nearly five million non-slaveholders among the whites. No non-slaveholder was known to be sent to Congress, ever became Governor of a Southern state, or was admitted to be a member of a Southern legislature. The whole of the South was therefore united under the control of these three or four hundred thousand slaveholders. Having crushed out every expression of dissent at home, they were able to govern the twenty-five or thirty millions of people at the North, by compelling both political parties to submit to their terms. Going on, step by step, they came at last to declare that slavery was not the evil their fathers had called it, but a blessing ; that the slaves were not wretched but happy ; that slavery was the corner-stone of free institutions ; that no republic could be sustained without resting on slavery ; and that it was sanctioned by the Bible itself. Yet all this time an inward sense of danger existed in every slaveholding community. There were two terrors constantly before the minds of Southern families —the dread of fire, and that of poison. These were the two weapons which the slaves had in their hands. When one of them had been abused, he might take his revenge on those who had wrought the wrong by setting fire to their houses or by putting poison into their food. I lived long at the South, and know that this was sometimes the case, and that nobody felt secure from these two dangers. Yet no newspaper was

ever allowed to mention it, when either of these events
occurred. You would never find in any Southern
paper the statement that a building had been burned
by slaves, or that a family had been poisoned. That
was kept strictly secret, lest it might become an example to others.

But there was one occasion in which these truths
came suddenly to light, and the hidden feelings of the
South were developed. It was when the Southampton
massacre occurred in 1831. Nat Turner, a slave, a
religious enthusiast, and, indeed, in reality a half-crazy
fanatic, formed a conspiracy to murder the white people and to give the power to the slaves. In this insurrection some sixty of the whites were killed, and
then the rebellion was conquered, and many of the
slaves were put to death. In the next Virginia legislature there was an outburst of feeling against slavery.
One member called slavery "a great blighting curse,"
and said "many a brave man, who will readily face
death in battle, has felt his blood chill, lest when he
went home at night he should find only the murdered
bodies of his family." Another declared that slavery
"was a mildew that had blighted every region it had
touched from the foundation of the world." Another
said, "I thank God that the spell is broken, and that
we now, for the first time, can say what we think. If
slavery can be eradicated, in God's name let us put an
end to it." Another declared, "I raise my voice for

emancipation. Tax us what you will. Prove us in
every way : but let us get rid of this horrid curse of
slavery." In reading what was said in that Virginia
legislature in this debate, in the year 1831, you would
have thought that you were attending a meeting of
abolitionists. Who would have supposed that this
same State of Virginia, in thirty years' time, would
have seceded from the Union in order to defend and
preserve this very institution ?

Abolitionists have stated the evils of slavery very
strongly, but they never have been overstated. It was
a condition of perpetual warfare. Not only were un-
told cruelties inflicted on the slaves almost as a matter
of necessity ; but among the whites, deeds of violence'
duels, street-shootings, death by lynch law, mob violence, in all its forms, were common. The young men
grew up in the midst of license and self-indulgences
of all kinds. It is true there were those who maintained their virtue ; there were upright, honorable
pure men and women of the South ; there were those
who respected the laws of God and man ; and they deserved all the more credit for acquiring and maintaining this character under such influences as those to
which they were exposed. There were, also, mistresses
and masters who felt a responsiblity for the care and
comfort of their slaves, and who devoted themselves
to those duties in the most praiseworthy manner. But

the system itself was so evil that it made their best efforts almost useless.

I, myself, was a citizen of the State of Kentucky from 1833 to 1840. Slavery existed there, it is true, in a comparatively mild form. But its evils were such that I learned to look on it with unmixed aversion. I learned my anti-slavery lessons from slavery itself and from the slaveholders around me. At that time I knew nothing of Mr. Garrison or his movement, and when I heard of him I supposed, as others did, that he was merely a violent fanatic. After I returned to Boston, in 1841, I had the advantage of knowing him and his fellow laborers, and seeing something of their grand and noble work.

But the sentiment of Kentucky, in those days, among all the better class of people, was that slavery was a wrong and an evil, and that it ought to be abolished. It was also believed that Kentucky would, when the time came for altering its Constitution, insert a clause in the new Constitution that would allow slavery to be abolished.

I will relate one or two anecdotes to show the feeling that prevailed at that time.

A young man from Boston called one day upon me in Louisville. He was a member of one of the very conservative families of New England, who believed that abolition was a fanatical movement, and that abolitionists were endangering the safety of the Union

He had been brought up with these sentiments. I took him with me to drive into the country to visit some of the plantations. The first place that we came to was the residence of Judge John J. Marshall, who belonged to one of the old families of Virginia and Kentucky. Mrs. Marshall was the sister of John G. Birney, afterwards candidate of the Free-Soil party for President. The Marshalls owned slaves, and there were a great many little negroes about the house. My Boston friend, seeing he was among slaveholders, thought it was a fitting opportunity for him to say something in favor of the institution. " Mrs. Marshall," said he, " I think our people at the North are very much mistaken in attacking slavery as they do. It seems to me there is nothing so very bad about it." Mrs. Marshall replied, "It will not do, sir, to defend slavery in *this* family. The Marshalls and the Birneys have always been abolitionists." He was a little surprised at that very decided statement, coming from slaveholders. We next drove to the house of my dear old friend, Judge John Speed, who had a large plantation and fifty or sixty slaves. He had the title of judge, not because he had ever studied law, for he had had very little opportunity for an education. But he was a very intelligent man—a man who had learned much by thinking and by observation. It was a custom at that time in Kentucky to appoint one or two men, whom they called associate judges, not law-

yers, to sit on the bench with the legal judge, in order
to keep him from indulging in the supposed quibbles
of the law ; and Judge Speed had been one of these
associate judges.

When we reached his house, he took us about the
plantation and showed us the negro cabins, having in
them various little comforts, such as muslin curtains
in the windows, pictures on the walls, or here and
there a piece of mahogany furniture. My friend from
Boston, thinking, no doubt, that Mrs. Marshall was
an exceptional person, and that he should be safe this
time in speaking in behalf of slavery, said, "Judge, I
do not see but the slaves are as happy as our laboring
classes at the North."

"Well," answered the Judge "I do the best I
can to make my slaves comfortable ; but I tell you
what it is, you cannot make a slave *happy*, do what
you will. God Almighty never meant a man to be a
slave, and he cannot be made happy while he is a
slave."

You may be sure that I felt proud and pleased
with my Kentucky friends.

But the Boston youth continued. "But what can
be done about it, sir ? They are not able to take
care of themselves, if they were free. How could they
manage if slavery were abolished ?"

"I think I could show you three men on my plantation," replied Judge Speed, "who might go to the

Kentucky legistature : I am inclined to believe they would make just as good legislators as the average men that you find there now."

In Kentucky in those days, it was not considered at all improper for a man to avow anti-slavery sentiments. I recollect we had a discussion in Louisville, which lasted three nights, in which we debated the whole question of slavery ; one side maintaining that it was right, and a good thing, and that it ought to be maintained ; and the other that it was an evil, socially morally and politically, and that it ought to be abolished. The majority were on the side of those who contended that it was an evil and a wrong. Nobody in the State thought that there was anything improper or dangerous in having the subject fully discussed. The Louisville Journal, then edited by Geo. D. Prentice, was ready to print articles pointing out the evils of slavery. I, myself, had a discussion in its columns with a St. Louis physician, who maintained that slavery was right, and that the negroes were little better than monkeys. Mr. Prentice printed my articles, and told me that he was glad to have them. At that time I edited a small monthly magazine, and I printed in it copious extracts from Dr. Channing's work on slavery. At the time of the Alton mob and the murder of Lovejoy, our " Western Messenger," printed in Louisville, took the ground that it was a murder, and a great disgrace to the

place where it occurred. No Kentuckian objected to
this being printed in Kentucky, although some of the
Alton people discontinued their subscriptions in consequence. In those days, every Kentuckian said that
Kentucky would be the first State to emancipate,
Alas! it was one of the very last. The question
why this was so is one which has a curious answer,
and one which throws light on human nature. The
truth was that Kentucky at that time was a Whig
State. It had been a Whig State for 15 years. The
Democrats had been driven from power in consequence of of committing the great mistake of trying
to abolish the old State Courts and substitute new
Courts, in order to maintain a State Bank, which the
Old Courts had declared contrary to to the Constitution of the United States. When it was found that
there were two Courts sitting, each claiming equal
jurisdiction, the people of the State were so indignant
with the Democratic party that it was turned out of
power at the next election. But fifteen years after,
when the convention was called to revise the Constitution, it so happened that the Democratic party had
been gradually gaining strength, till it was nearly
equal in voters to the Whig party. When the question was brought forward as to whether an anti-slavery
clause should be inserted in the Constitution, each of
these two great parties was afraid to do anything
about it. They knew that it ought to be done, but

they were afraid of the injury that might come to their respective parties from doing it, and so neither of them accepted the issue. There were, however, at that time, a small number of genuine anti-slavery people in the State. Among them was Robert J. Breckenridge, one of the most eminent clergymen in the South, and noted for his hostility to slavery. He took the stump at Lexington, and offered to discuss the question of abolition, and to defend emancipation in the State; and for three days he spoke to the crowds that assembled before the Lexington Court House, He held to his convictions to the last, even after the war broke out, though his nephew, the Vice-President of the United States, became a leader of the Confederates.

Among the great evils of slavery were the acts of violence produced by it. When I went to Kentucky duelling was considered entirely proper and neces, sary. I preached a sermon against it on the occasion of a very extraordinary duel which had just taken place, and the father of one of the combatants, who had been a U. S. Senator, Judge Rowan, was in the church that day. He said that he " could not understand what had got into Mr. Clark's head to preach against duelling. He might as well preach against courage."

The occasion of that duel, and the character of it was so remarkable, that I may as well speak of it to indicate something of the spirit of the South at that time.

The judges of the courts in Kentucky were paid such very small salaries, that one could seldom find a lawyer of any eminence who would consent to accept the office. Consequently the judges knew very little about law, and were not much respected by the bar. The judge of the district where I lived was one of this inferior class, and the bar did not pay him proper respect. But he was a man of a good deal of pride, and on one occasion, when he had been grossly insulted by a lawyer, he ordered the offender to be sent to jail for twenty-four hours for contempt of court. Thereupon the rest of the lawyers said they would go there too ; so they all went to the upper chamber of the jail, where they had a supper, and spent the night in carousing together. During the night a little quarrel occurred, during which a young man by the name of Howells threw some wine on Tom Marshall's coat. This called for a challenge. They went across the river and had their duel in Indiana, but it was understood that it need not be a deadly one. After exchanging shots the matter was adjusted, and Marshal, to show that he had spared his opponent, fired his remaining pistol at a little sapling, and the bark flew from the tree. The second of his opponent, who did not like Marshall, then remarked : " It is a little strange that you should be able to hit a tree at that distance

and not be able to hit a man who is much nearer."
" If *you* were the man standing opposite to me I should
be able to hit you," returned Marshall. " I will give
you an opportunity whenever you choose," was the
reply. It was then arranged that they should go out
and fight each other. As it was understood that they
were the best shots in the city, it was supposed that
both might be killed. As Mr. Rowan was rather I
better shot than Marshall, it was thought that the
latter ought to have an opportunity to practise, and
the duel was postponed for a fortnight to give him an
opportunity.

Every day Marshall rode into the country after
breakfast, and practised an hour or two at a mark.
Meanwhile a ball was given at Judge Rowan's, and
both opponents were present. At that time John
Howard Payne was on a visit in Louisville, and he
frequently came to see me at my lodgings. He entered my room one morning and said, " I have travelled
a great deal, and seen a great variety of customs, but
I have never met with anything exactly like this
society of yours in Kentucky. I was at the ball last
night, and saw Mr. Marshall dancing with a lady to
whom he is supposed to be engaged, and opposite him
was Mr. Rowan with his lady. Every one knew that
they were going out in a few days to fight a deadly
duel with each other, but nothing showed itself on
the surface." The duel took place, and Mr. Rowan

fired a little more quickly than his opponent. His ball hit Marshall on the hip and made him lame during his after life.

Peaceful emancipation had long been hoped for. Gradual emancipation was expected by the fathers of the nation—Washington, Jefferson, Madison. But the prosperity of the South had grown so great through slavery, that emancipation became ever more difficult. The cotton crop had reached such vast dimensions that slavery brought great prosperity to the South, and instead of being willing to free the slaves they had, they wanted more.

I was at Henry Clay's home, a. Ashland, about the year 1837. He had been riding ever his estate on horseback, and came back tired, and lay down on the sofa and talked to me about slavery. He said he had hoped to see the end of it at least in Kentucky, but cotton had become so profitable that the Southern States would not give it up. Production had greatly increased, but the demand had increased still more rapidly. He had expected to see the supply overlap the demand, but the contrary took place. Cotton planters and sugar planters made money so fast that the price of slaves had greatly increased.

I once met a young man from Pittsburg, who was a decided Presbyterian, and at the same time a strong anti-slavery man. I asked him how he became so. He said that in his church in Pittsburg, most of the members defended slavery, and he had supposed it was all right until he once travelled in Virginia. He was riding on the outside of the stage-coach, sitting with the driver. On the top of the coach there was a young colored boy, perhaps 18 or 19 years old. When they came to a cross-road, he said to the driver, " I get off here, master ; this is as far as I go. I get off here." " No you don't," said the driver. " Yes I do. I get off here to go and see my old grandmother. Master said so." " No, you are not going to see her, you are going with me," replied the driver. As soon as he gave that answer the boy understood that he was sent to be sold South, and that he had been de- ceived about it so that there should be no disturbance about his going away. He would never see his home or friends again. He burst into an anguish, an agony of tears, and cried so bitterly that the heart of the driver was touched, and he said to the young man sit- ting beside him, " Damn them ! I wish they would give their devilish work to somebody else to do," and I think the recording angel dropped a tear on that oath. As it happened, when he looked round after a while, the boy had disappeared. " I am glad he has gone," said the driver, " but I suppose I must stop and pretend to look for him." So he stopped a little while and then drove on.

That single fact converted this young Presbyterian to anti-slavery ; but this case must be multiplied by ten thousand other instances to show the amount of suffering and misery from that single source—the separation of families.  It was said that ten thousand slaves were sold every year from Virginia to the cotton States.

I was once in Baltimore with a friend who was rather conservative, and who thought that the abolitionists were going too far and too fast.  He went to a party one night, and when he came home he said to me : " I think that I may become an abolitionist myself."  " How is that ? " I asked.  " At this party they pointed out to me a lady dressed in rich costume, evidently a very fashionable person, and they told me she derived her support by being the owner of some half dozen married negro women whose husbands were owned by other persons.  The children were hers because she owned the mothers, and she derived her income from the sale of these children, disposing of them as fast as they came to an age at which they would bring a good amount.  I do not think," said he, " I can stand a system that produces such results."

Now came the time when the stone cut of the mountain, without hands, was to strike this idol and cause it to fall.

On the evening of January 6th, an event took place in Boston which few of the inhabitants knew anything about, and the importance of which no one suspected. A fierce snowstorm was raging ; the snow mixed with sleet and rain, and the streets hardly passable. On that dismal night a few men assembled in the African Baptist Church, on Belknap street. Then and there was organized the Anti-Slavery Society, which was like the little mustard seed of the Bible, destined to grow in power and influence till its great object was attained. Those present were David Lee Child, William Snelling, William Lloyd Garrison, Ellis Gray Loring, Oliver Johnson, Samuel E. Sewall, Arnold Buffum and a few others. Twelve signed the constitution. "Not many wise, not many noble" joined their ranks ; but then, as often, God chose the weak things of the world to confound the mighty, and things that were not, to bring to nought things that were.

William Lloyd Garrison, the leader of this movement, was endowed with the qualities necessary for a reformer. His intellect was clear and logical ; his purpose determined ; he had an iron will, and convictions which when once formed knew no doubt and no shadow of turning. To him right was right and wrong was wrong, and he saw no half lights or half shadows between the two. He always called a spade a spade, and did not define it as an agricultural instrument commonly used to alter the position of the soil. His conscience was despotic, and was in the closest alliance with his convictions. Evil to his mind was inexcusable, intolerable. All the old puritan hatred of sin was in him, joined with all the puritan inability to comprehend how there could be a sin without a sinner. In 1832 he was only 27 years old, and had already been confined in jail for his anti-slavery writings. He established his paper, " The Liberator," January 1st, 1831, without a subscriber, and without a dollar of capital. He and his associate printed it themselves ; they lived on bread from the baker, and slept in the printing office, which was in the third story of the building. Oliver Johnson describes the dingy walls ; the windows and floors bespattered with ink ; the press in one corner, the composing stands opposite ; the writing-table covered with newspapers ; the bed of the editor and publisher on the floor. Lowell also pictures the scene ; quoting at the head of the poem this passage from the letter of Harrison Gray Otis, then Major of Boston :—

" Some time afterward it was reported to me by the city officers that they had ferreted out the paper and its editor ; that his office was an obscure hole, his only visible auxiliary a negro boy, and his supporters a very few insignificent persons of all colors.

> " In a small chamber, friendless and unseen,
>   Toiled o'er his types one poor unlearned young man.
>   The place was dark, unfurnitured and mean,
>   Yet there the freedom of a race began.

> "O Truth ! O freedom ! low are ye, still born
>   In the rude stable, in the manger nursed ;

What humble hands unbar those gates of morn
Through which the splendors of the new day burst.

" Shall we not heed the lesson taught of old,
  And by the Present's lips repeated still,
In our own single manhood to be bold,
  Fortressed in conscience and impregnable will.

" O small beginnings, ye are great and strong,
  Based on a faithful heart and weariless brain—
Ye build the future fair, ye conquer wrong,
  Ye earn the crown, and wear it not in vain."

Before that crown was won there was a long strug
gle to go through, and many bitter disappointments
to encounter. But Garrison held to his purpose to
the end—the purpose he announced at the beginning.
He was thought by many to be too harsh ; too severe ;
too denunciatory. And certainly he choose his words
with the careful purpose of making them shock and
sting. His programme was this : " I will be as harsh
as truth, as uncompromising as justice. . . . I am in
earnest ; I will not equivocate ; I will not excuse ; I
will not retreat a single inch, and I will be heard."

I remember once hearing that when George Brad-
burn was told that he ought not to call slaveholders
thieves and robbers, as he was in the habit of doing,
he replied, " If I should go to the stall of that old
apple-woman and take away her apples, you would
call me a thief ; but if I were to take not only the
apples, but the old woman herself, you think it would
be wrong to say I was a robber."

Mr. Garrison's paper very soon roused a nest of hornets. The State of Georgia offered a reward of $5,000 for his arrest and conviction. Similiar offers, sincere or fictitious, were made by other Southern States. Then came a period of mobs. There were mobs all over the North, wherever the anti-slavery missionaries went. July 4th, 1834, there was a mob in New York, when the house of Louis Tappan was sacked. At the same time, the schoolhouses and churches of colored people were attacked and damaged. August 13th, in the same year, there was a terrible riot in Philadelphia, that continued for three nights. Forty-four houses of colored people were damaged and destroyed. Many colored people were beaten and cruelly injured, and some were killed.

In the year 1835, Rev. Samuel J. May was mobbed five times in Vermont. If there was ever a man, at the same time perfectly courageous and straightforward, and also sweet-tempered and fair to his opponents, it was Samuel Joseph May. One would suppose him to be the last man to be mobbed. October 21, 1835, there was a riot in Utica, and another on the same day in the city of Boston, when the meeting of the Women's Anti-Slavery Society was broken up, and Garrison was carried through the streets with a rope around his body. He was protected by Major Lyman, and put in jail for safety. On the same day, a convention of six hundred delegates met at Utica

and formed an Anti Slavery Society. They were
shut out of the Court House by a mob, then went
into a meeting house, but the assembly was broken-
up, and they were driven away with much violence·
On the 17 of May, 1838, Penn Hall, built by the
friends of free discussion at a cost of $40,000, and dedi-
cated on May 14th, was burned by a mob. Colored
orphan asylums and churches were, at the same time,
attacked and damaged.

Amid these scenes the Anti-Slavery Society held
on its way. Their cause gained more and more in
power. Good and able men and women were converted to it. The more it was attacked the more it
grew.

In 1838, there were issued from the Anti-Slavery
office in New York, 646,000 copies of its various
publications. During a five months session of Congress, petitions were sent to it for the abolition of
slavery in the District of Columbia, signed by 400,000
persons. In two years, more than two million signa-
tures were obtained to these petitions.

The poets were largely on the side of the reform.
Such writers as William Cullen Bryant, John Pierpont, James Russell Lowell, Henry W. Longfellow,
and more than all, John G. Whittier, gained some of
their best laurels in this struggle.

The American Colonization Society, first organized
in 1816, was advocated with great zeal as the wise

method of removing slavery from the country. The slaves were to be gradually emancipated and sent back to Africa, where they were to act as missionaries of religion and civilization. But its course was inconsistent and illogical. At the North it offered itself as the true means to abolish slavery. At the South it proposed to make slavery more secure by sending away the free colored people, who were a source of danger to the institution. Regarded simply as a missionary society, it was unobjectionable, except from the natural difficulties in its way. But as a means of removing slavery, its plans were absurd. In 1840, the annual increase of the negroes in the United States was about 40,000, to remove whom to Africa, at the low estimate of $100 each, would take $4,000,-000. But how were they to live after reaching that deadly coast ? To take two or three millions of laborers from the place where their labor was needed and valuable, and transfer them to a place where there was no demand for it, surely seemed the most chimerical of schemes. As such, it was exposed by Garrison and his friends, and those friends of the slave who had been misled by its claims were undeceived.*

— *A pamphlet published in 1881, by Geo. R. Stetson, of Boston, called " The Liberian Republic as it is," informs us that there are only about 20,000 American emigrants and their descendants now in Liberia; that the climate is deadly, the people poor, and that there is not a horse, and only one plough in the colony.

## CHAPTER II.

### THE FIGHT IN CONGRESS.

"They are slaves who dare not be
In the right with two or three."
LOWELL.

As when, before a violent thunderstorm, low rumbling sounds are heard from time to time below the horizon, announcing its coming ; so before the great anti-slavery fight in Congress there were occasional indications from time to time of the approaching tempest. Such were the debates in 1797, in which one very brave and loyal man, who is not much remembered I fear, took a distinguished part. This was George Thacher, a member of Congress from Massachusetts. Through many years, all the time that he was in Congress, he opposed openly and decidedly, with all his heart and soul, the aggressions of the slave-power. Such were the conflicts also in which Josiah Quincy took a prominent part. He was one of the very first to foresee the struggle which freedom and the North would be obliged to wage with the slave-power of the South. To the end of his extreme old age, as long as he lived, he was faithful to the cause of freedom. I have a note from him, written only a month or two before his death, with which he sent me his check in behalf of some effort for the benefit of the colored people. Such also was the contest which ended with the Missouri compromise in 1820, and the admis ion of the State of Missouri into the Union as a slave state.

In all these battles the slave-power won the victory by its strength of will, its vehement threats and its compact unity of purpose. The word "slave-power" was first used by John Gorham Palfrey, who characterized by this very appropriate name that vast political force united and made compact by slavery.

Occasionally, however, the Southern fire-eaters would meet with stern resistance from Northern men. So the sea on our coast, with its stormy waves, beats against the old granite rocks of the shore of New England. Such firm opposition they met in Josiah Quincy, and I think they liked him the better for it. Another Northern man who never feared to encounter them, was Tristram Burges, of Rhode Island. He was full of humor and full of pluck. Many stories are told of his retorts when he was in conflict with Southern men during the years from 1825 to 1835.

Passing by these preliminary skirmishes between slavery and freedom, we come down to 1835, when the real battle commenced on the floor of Congress,

which ended in the secession of the Southern members.

The question found its way into the debates of
Congress in the form of petitions for the abolition of
slavery and the slave trade in the District of Columbia.
If the slaveholders had allowed these petitions to be
received and referred, taking no notice of them, it
seems probable that no important results would have
followed. But, blinded by rage and fear, they opposed
their reception, thus denying a privilege belonging to
all mankind,—that of asking the government to redress
their grievances. Then came to the front a man
already eminent by his descent, his great attainments,
his long public service, his great position, and his
commanding ability. John Quincy Adams, after
having been President of the United States, accepted
a seat in the House of Representatives, and was one
of the most laborious and useful of its members. He
was not then an Abolitionist, nor in favor even of
abolishing slavery in the District of Columbia. But
he believed that the people had the right to petition
the government for anything they desired, and that
their respectful petitions should be respectfully received. Sixty-five years old in 1832, when he began
this conflict, his warfare with the slave-power ended
only when, struck with death while in his seat, he
"saw the last of earth and was content." With what
energy, what dauntless courage, what untiring industry,

what matchless powers of argument, what inexhaustible
resources of knowledge, he pursued his object, the
future historian of the struggle will take pleasure in
describing.

At first there were only two or three Northern men
who stood against the slave-power.  John Quincy
Adams was for many years almost alone in the House
of Representatives, and John P. Hale, for some years
was alone in the Senate.  The character and career
of John Quincy Adams are both  equally remarkable.
He had immense ability, perfect integrity, and a spot-
less reputation.  There was no better illustration of
his character than those famous lines of Horace about
the just man, who is tenacious of his purpose, and
able to hold himself equally against the stormy mob
and the imperious tyrant.  He had vast industry, a
great store of knowledge, a keen and penetrating in-
sight into men and things.   He was respected, but
not much liked.   He possessed little power of entering into sympathetic relations with others.  I suppose
that he was one of the most lonely men of his time.
His was a temper easily roused to anger ; and he was
full of dislikes and distastes.  There was no more
dangerous antagonist than this man, in whom the rage
for battle was ready to kindle at once into an inex-
tinguishable fire.

I recollect that I was once sitting in the parlor of
the Louisville Hotel, in Kentucky, somewhere about

1835 or 1836, when I heard a conversation about John Quincy Adams between two Southern statesmen, Felix Grundy of Tennessee, and Gov. Pondexter, of Missouri. They talked about various subjects, and among the rest about Adams. One of them said, " Our Southern friends in the House find it impossible to do anything with that old man. They cannot contrive any way by which to put him down. If they wish to get any measure through, which he will be likely to oppose, they try to find a time to do it when he is not there ; but there is no such time, because he is always in his place. There is no use in questioning his facts, because he is always right. His memory never fails him. He is a very difficult man to argue with, because he always grows keener and sharper with every attack. At one time they thought it would be a good plan to neglect him, to talk with each other, and pay no attention while he was speaking ; but the truth is, he is so infinitely interesting, that it is impossible not to listen to him whenever he begins to speak—and every one crowds closer to his chair so as not to lose a word."

Adams was born in 1767 ; the son of a president, and a president himself, he passed through every scene of public life before he entered into the last, which was the most important of all. When he was eleven years old he went with his father to Paris. He began his diary in 1779, at the age of twelve, and ended it in 1848, just before his death, at the age of 81. In 1794 he was sent ambassador to Holland ; in 1797 to Berlin. In 1802 he returned, and was elected a member of the Massachusetts legislature. The next year he was elected to the United States Senate. In 1809, he went as minister to Russia. In 1814 he signed the treaty of peace with Great Britain with the other Commissioners. In 1815 he became Ambassador at the Court of St. James. In 1817, he was appointed Secretary of State to President Monroe. In 1825 he became president, and after four years was superseded by Andrew Jackson. Then, at 63 years of age, he appeared to have run the whole round of political experience. He, himself thought that his career was over ; but in fact, it had only just begun. Disliked by the old Federalists and leading statesmen in Massachusetts, when nominated for governor and afterwards for senator, he was defeated each time by John Davis, and seemed to have no more opportunity. But the citizens of the district in which he lived nominated him for Congress in 1830.

I recollect that at this time his old and warm friend, Josiah Quincy, came over to Newton to see my grandfather, James Freeman, and talk with him about this nomination. Mr. Quincy was strongly convinced that it was a mistake on the part of John Quincy Adams to go to Congress. His argument was that a man who had been president had acquired an influence which he ought to reserve to use on some great occasion, and not to have it frittered away by debates in Congress. He believed that Mr. Adams should retire and be quiet, until there came some very important crisis, when he might use his reserved influence to advantage. Mr. Quincy was very earnest in this argument. My grandfather said little until he had got through, and then only remarked, " I have always thought that the best way to keep one's influence is to *use* it." That was singularly the case with John Quincy Adams. He went to Congress and used his influence, which continued to increase to the last.

At this time, the Northern abolitionists sent petitions to Congress for the abolition of slavery in the District of Columbia. They contended that as this territory was under the control of the United States' Government, the United States was responsible for slavery there ; and that the Free States were bound to do what they could to have slavery brought to an end in that District. But the Slave States were not willing to have anything said on the subject, so they passed what was called a " gag " law in the House of Representatives, and ruled that all petitions which had any relation to slavery should be laid on the table without being debated, printed or referred. John Quincy Adams opposed this rule resolutely, maintaining that it was wrong and unconstitutional. He said, when the resolution was about to pass, " I hold this resolution to be a practical violation of the

Constitution of the United States, of the rules of this House, and of the rights of my constitutents." Notwithstanding this protest, it was passed by a vote of 117 to 68. But whenever the rule came up to be renewed he repeated the same declaration, and insisted on his answer being entered in the journal. When he was called upon to vote "yes" or "no" on the resolution, he refused to vote, but made the same statement, that he held the resolution to be in direct violation of the Constitution, etc. The speaker told him that this was not a vote, and that it could not be entered in the journal. Mr. Adams then requested that his statement, with the Speaker's decision, that it was not a vote, should both be entered in the journal. He continued to present petitions, as before, for the abolition of slavery in the District. When the day came for petitions he was one of the first to be called upon ; and he would sometimes occupy nearly the whole hour in presenting them, though each one was immediately laid on the table. One day he presented 511. There came a day, Monday, February 6, 1836, when there was one of the most extraordinary scenes which, I think, ever took place in any deliberative body. There are few scenes in the history of such assemblies to compare with the dramatic character of that scene, in which, John Quincy Adams, for several days stood alone against a great tumultuous crowd of slaveholders, attempting in every way to have him expelled or censured, and in which Mr. Adams got the **victory** over them all. Adams rose in his seat, and **said** he had in his possession a paper on which he desired the decision of the Speaker as to whether it would come under the rule of the House respecting subjects concerning slavery. " I hold in my hand," said he, " a petition from twenty persons professing to be slaves in Virginia. Does this come under the rules or not, Mr. Speaker?" "Send it to me," said the Speaker, "and I will decide upon it." "No," said Mr. Adams, "if it were sent to you it would then be in possession of the House : and I do not propose to present it to the House until I have the decision. It may be an imposition." Immediately there rose a most violent uproar, and cries of " Censure him ! Censure him! " " Expel him ! " Haynes, of Georgia, cried out that it must not be received. Mr. Dixon Lewis, of Alabama, said that Mr. Adams ought to be punished for offering such a petition. He added that the Southern members ought to leave the House in a body. Others cried out that Adams ought to be expelled. Thompson, of South Carolina, moved that Mr. Adams was guilty of gross disrespect to the House, and that he be brought to the bar to receive severe censure for offering this petition. Another Southern member moved that Mr. Adams had rendered himself liable to censure, and is hereby censured, for presenting a petition from slaves. Then Mr. Dixon Lewis moved, " That, whereas, John Ouincy

Adams, by his attempt to introduce a petition from slaves for the abolition of slavery in the District of Columbia, has committed an outrage ; and as by this flagrant conduct he will excite the slaves to insurrecrection, he has laid himself liable to censure."

Then Mr. Adams rose and said very frankly, " I wish to save the House from wasting its time on resolutions founded on a mistake. The gentleman from Alabama had better amend his resolution to make it conform with facts. In the first place I have not attempted to introduce a petition. I merely said I had one in my possession, and asked what should be done with it. And, moreover, there is nothing in the petition about the abolition of slavery in the District, but something very different from that. It is something which would please the gentlemen who have attacked me much better than it would suit me."

Then Mr. Adams sat down, leaving his opponents more angry than before, but somewhat confused. Mr. Waddy Thompson modified his resolution, putting it in this form : That Mr. Adams be censured for " creating the impression, and leaving the House under the impression, that the petition was for the abolition of slavery in the District of Columbia." " But," said Mr. Adams, " I certainly ought not to be censured for your mistakes, or for your follies." After a multitude of other speeches from the enraged

Southern chivalry the debate of the first day came to
an end.

On the next day (February 7), in reply to a question, Mr. Adams stated again that he had not attempted to present the petition, though his own feelings
would have led him to do so, but had kept it in his
possession, out of respect to the House. He had
said nothing to lead the House to infer that this peti
tion was for the abolition of slavery. He should consider before presenting a petition from slaves ; though,
in his opinion, slaves had a right to petition, and the
mere fact of a petition being from slaves would not
of itself prevent him from presenting it. If the petition was a proper one, he should present it. A petition was a prayer, a supplication to a superior being.
Slaves might pray to God : was this House so superior that it could not condescend to hear a prayer from
those to whom the Almighty listened ? He ended
by saying that, in asking the question of the Speaker,
he had intended to show the greatest respect to
the House, and had not the least purpose of trifling
with it.

These brief remarks of Mr. Adams made it necessary for the slaveholders again to change their tactics.
Mr. Dromgoole, of Virginia, now brought forward his
famous resolution, which Mr. Adams afterwards made
so ridiculous, accusing him of having " given color to
an idea " that slaves had a right to petition, and that

he should be censured by the Speaker for this act.
Another member proposed, rather late in the day,
that a committee be appointed to inquire whether
any attempt had been made, or not, to offer a petition
from slaves. Another offered a series of resolutions,
declaring that if any one " hereafter " should offer
petitions from slaves, he ought to be regarded as an
enemy of the South, and of the Union ; but that " as
John Quincy Adams had stated that he meant no
disrespect to the House, that all proceedings as to
his conduct should now cease." And so, after
many other speeches, the second day's debate came
to an end.

The next day was set apart to count the votes for
President, and so the debate was resumed February
9. It soon became more confused than ever. Mo-
tions were made to lay the resolutions on the table ;
they were withdrawn ; they were renewed ; they
were voted down ; and, finally, after much discussion, and when at last the final question was about
being taken, Mr. Adams inquired whether he was to
be allowed to be heard in his own defence before being condemned. So he obtained the floor, and immediately the whole aspect of the case was changed.
During three days he had been the prisoner at the
bar ; suddenly he became the judge on the bench.
Never, in the history of forensic eloquence, has a
single speech effected a greater change in the pur-

pose of a deliberative assembly. Often as the Hora-
tion description has been quoted of the just man,
tenacious of his purpose, who fears not the rage of
citizens clamoring for what is wrong, it has never
found a fitter application than to the unshaken mind
of John Quincy Adams, standing alone, in the midst
of his antagonists, like a solid monument which the
idle storms beat against in vain.

He began by saying that he had been waiting during these three days for an answer to the question
which he had put to the Speaker, and which the
Speaker had put to the House, but which the House
had not yet answered, namely, whether the paper he
held in his hand came under the rule of the House or
not. They had discussed everything else, but had
not answered that question. They had wasted the
time of the House in considering how they could censure him for doing what he had not done. All he
wished to know was, whether a petition from slaves
should be received or not. He himself thought that
it ought to be received ; but if the House decided
otherwise he should not present it. Only one gentleman had undertaken to discuss that question, and his
argument was, that if slavery was abolished by Congress in any State, you violated the Constitution ;
and, *therefore*, slaves ought not to be allowed to petition for anything. He, Mr. Adams, was unable to

see the connection between the premises and the conclusion.

(Hereupon poor Mr. French, the author of this argument, tried to explain what he meant by it, but left his meaning as confused as before.)

Then Mr. Adams added, that if you deprive any one in the community of the right of petition, which is only the right of offering a prayer, you will find it difficult to know where to stop: one gentleman had objected to the reception of one petition, because offered by women of a bad character. Mr. Patton, of Virginia, says he *knows* that one of the names is of a woman of a bad character.

(Hereupon Mr. Patton explained that he did not himself know the woman, but had been told that her character was not good.)

" So," said Mr. Adams, " you first deny the right of petition to slaves, then to free people of color, and then you inquire into the moral character of a petitioner before you receive his petition. The next step will be to inquire into the political belief of the petitioners before you receive their petition." Mr. Robertson, of Virginia, had said that no petition ought to be received for an object which Congress had no power to grant. Mr. Adams replied, with much acuteness, that on most questions the right of granting the petition might be in doubt: a majority must decide that point: it would therefore follow, from Mr.

Robertson's rule, that no one had a right to petition
unless he belonged to the predominant party. Mr.
Adams then turned to Mr. Dromgoole, who had
charged him with the remarkable crime of "giving
color to an idea," and soon made that representative
of the Old Dominion appear very ridiculous.

Mr. Adams then proceeded to rebuke, with dignity
but severity, the conduct of those who had proposed to
censure him without any correct knowledge of the facts
of the case. His criticisms had the effect of compelling
these gentlemen to excuse themselves and to offer
various explanations of their mistakes. These assailants suddenly found themselves in an attitude of self-
defence. Mr. Adams graciously accepted their explanations, advising them in future to be careful when
they undertook to offer resolutions of censure. He
then informed Mr. Waddy Thompson, of South Carolina, that he had one or two questions to put to him.
by this time it had become a pretty serious business
to receive the attentions of Mr. Adams ; and Mr.
Waddy Thompson immediately rose to explain. But
Mr. Adams asked him to wait until he had fully stated
the question which Mr. Thompson was to answer.
The southern statesmen had threatened the ex-President of the United States with an indictment by the
grand jury of the District for words spoken in debate
in the House of Representatives, and had added that,
if the petition was presented, Mr. Adams should be

The truth was that no one then knew the amount of patriotism in the heart of the northern people. When the New York Herald said that the City of New York would go with the seceders, it did not seem such a very improbable statement. The business of New York was largely with the South. The city was in the hands of the Democratic party. The negro was hated there by the rabble. Anti-slavery had scarcely obtained a foothold with the mass of the people. The events which were to follow the attack on Fort Sumter ; the great uprising of the North ; the tide of patriotic devotion which would sweep over every Northern State and city, silencing all opposition and making disunion odious, was all hidden alike from friends and foes. The slave-power hoped for an easy and unresisted triumph. The friends of human liberty apprehended that to prevent secession the North would give up the last defences of freedom, justice and humanity.

If the South had seceded peacefully ; if it had not attacked our forts and troops, but had simply taken a negative position towards the United States, refusing to send members to Congress, I think after a while we should have been obliged to allow them to form a separate and independent state. Mr. Seward and his friends were seeking how to make concessions. He had great faith in compromises, and was very anxious that something should be done. He was one of those

but they had brought themselves by a series of violent harangues, into a condition of bitter excitement
against him. When he ended, the effect of this extraordinary speech was such, that all the resolutions
were rejected, and out of the whole House only
twenty-two members could be found to pass a vote of
even indirect censure. The victory was won, and won
by Mr. Adams almost single-handed. We count
Horatius Cocles a hero for holding the Roman
bridge against a host of enemies; but greater honors
belong to him who successfully defends against over-
whelming numbers the ancient safeguards of public
liberty. For this reason we have repeated here at
such length the story of three days which the people
of the United States ought always to remember. It
took ten years to accomplish the actual repeal of these
gag-laws. But the main work was done when the
right of speech was obtained for the friends of freedom in Congress ; and John Quincy Adams was the
great leader in this warfare.*

Although in these debates, Mr. Adams bore the
brunt of the battle alone, and was perfectly equal to
doing it, there were a few members of the House, and
the Senate, who stood by his side in the defence of
the Right of Petition. Mr. Lincoln and Caleb Cush-
ing, of Massachusetts ; Mr. Evans, of Maine ; Wil-

* This account has been taken, by permission, from an article in the
North American Review, written by the author of the present work.

liam Slade, of Vermont ; and in the Senate, Morris, of Ohio, stood firm for this right.

But the most courageous supporter of Mr. Adams in Congress, and the most determined opponent of the slave-power, was Joshua R. Giddings of Ohio. Born in Pennsylvania, he was taken by his parents, when he was ten years old, to Ashtabula County, in the Western Reserve in Ohio. This region had been settled from New England, and its inhabitants were an intelligent and energetic people, believing in freedom and humanity. It was strongly anti-slavery. Elected to Congress in 1838, Giddings immediately placed himself by the side of Mr. Adams as a prominent defender of the Right of Petition, and an opponent of the pro-slavery party. In 1842, he brought before Congress the case of the Creole, an American vessel, which sailed from Virginia for New Orleans with a cargo of 136 slaves. The slaves rose against the master and crew, and took the ship into the British port of Nassau, where their right to freedom was recognized. This event created much excitement, and Mr. Webster, then Secretary of State, in a letter to Edward Everett, then Minister in London, declared the intention of our Government to demand indemnification for the owners. Mr. Giddings maintained, in a series of resolutions offered in Congress, that slavery being an abridgment of natural right, could have no force beyond the territorial jurisdiction which created it, and that a vessel leaving the United States and passing upon the high seas, left slavery behind. Consequently the slaves had become free, and had violated no law in seizing their freedom, and that we had no claim to any indemnity. For taking this ground, the House voted to censure Mr. Giddings. Thereupon he resigned his seat and appealed to his constituents, who re-elected him by a large majority. He was re-elected again and again during twenty-one years. During all this period he was one of the most determined and plucky opponents of the slave-power, and consequently was the subject of frequent abuse and threats. This, however, made no impression on this sturdy Ohio abolitionist, a meet companion of Corwin, Morris, Chase, and Root of that noble State.

Jan. 21, 1842, Mr. Adams presented a petition from 45 citizens of Haverhill, Mass., praying for the dissolution of the Union, and moved it be referred to a select committee, with instructions to report why the petition should not be granted. There was at once great excitement and members called out, "Expel him," "Censure him." After a good deal of fruitless endeavor to accomplish something, the House adjourned, and forty or fifty slaveholders met to decide what kind of resolutions should be presented to meet the case. Thomas F. Marshall of Kentucky was selected by this caucus from Congress to propose the resolutions, which were to the effect that for present-

ing such a petition to a body each of whom had taken
an oath to maintain the Constitution, Mr. Adams was
virtually inviting them to prejure themselves, and
that therefore he deserved the severest censure.
Marshall supported this with a very violent speech.
Mr. Wise followed in another. Then Mr. Adams
arose and asked the clerk to read the first paragraph
of the Declaration of Independence being the one
which recognizes the right of every people to alter or
abolish their form of Government when it ceases to
accomplish its ends. He said that those who believed
that the present Government was oppressive had the
right (according to the Declaration of Independence,
on which the whole of our national unity reposes), to
petition Congress to do what they believed was desirable ; and all that Congress could properly do would
be to explain to them why such an act could not be
performed. He replied with great ,severity to Mr.
Wise and said that Mr. Wise had come into that Hall
a few years before with his hands dripping with the
blood of one of his fellow beings. In this he alluded
to the part which Mr. Wise had taken in the duel between Mr. Graves of Kentucky, and Cilley of Maine,
in which the latter had been killed. As for Mr. Marshall who had accused him of treason, he spoke of him
with great scorn. " I thank God! " said he " that
the Constitution of my country has defined treason,
and has not left it to the puny intellect of this young

man from Kentucky to say what it is. If I were the
father of this gentleman from Kentucky, I should
take him from this House and put him to school where
he might study his profession for some years until he
became a little better qualified to appear in this place."
Mr. Adams had on his desk a great many books and
references prepared for his use by some anti-slavery
gentlemen then in Washington ; after he had gone
on for some time with his speech he was asked how
much more time he would probably occupy. He replied " I believe Mr. Burke took three months for his
speech on Warren Hasting's indictment. I think I
may probably get through in ninety days, perhaps in
less time." Thereupon they thought it just as well to
have the whole thing come to an end and it was
moved that the matter should be laid on the table.
Mr. Adams consented, and it was done.

In these two cases he defeated his enemies in a
hand to hand fight. After this they had so much respect for him, that on one occasion when the house
met and found itself unable to organize, on account
of the clerk's refusing to read the names of certain
members from New Jersey who had received their
Governor's certificate but whose seats were contested,
Mr. Adams was asked if he could point out a way by
which the House could be organized. He replied
" Yes, I, myself, will call you to order if you will
allow me to do so," Thereupon he said, " I call on you

to come to order and I ask you to nominate a temporary speaker." He was himself chosen the temporary speaker and for several days presided over the House until they were able to appoint a permanent speaker. His career in Congress is very interesting, showing that at his advanced age he still preserved all this wonderful power and was more than a match for his opponents. His firmness was stronger than their violence, for he had justice and right with him. He was a man of such invincible tenacity of purpose that with the right on his side he was perfectly invulnerable. He could not be defeated.

I have spoken of John P. Hale, who was a very different man. He was a Democrat, chosen by New Hampshire as member of the House of Representatives. While there the project of the annexation of Texas came up, and he opposed it. He went back to New Hampshire and continued to oppose this plan, which had become a party measure to which the Democrats had committed themselves. He took the stump through the whole state showing the evil and wrong of annexation, the object of which was the increase of the slave-power. He succeeded in changing the sentiments of the people on this subject to such a degree that in the course of the year he was returned to the Senate as an Independent Democrat. He was there for several years alone, with no one to stand by him, being elected to the Senate in 1847. He was prompt, ready, quick, able to answer any attack at a moment's warning. He had the faculty of thinking on his feet. He also possessed a large fund of good humor and much genuine wit. He was good at repartee, and though the slaveholders did their best to put him down, they seldom got the better of him.

In the winter of 1851 and 1852, I was in Washington and was frequently on the floor of the Senate chamber, during this session, which was the last attended by Henry Clay. The compromises as they were called, had been passed, the compromises by which the Free Soil party was to be put down and Political anti-slavery was to be brought to an end. All anti-slavery discussion was also expected to cease, and the whole excitement about slavery to be ended. Mr. Clay rose one day in his place, and speaking of the Free Soil party said, " It has been put down ; *down, down, down;* so low that it will never rise again. I thank God that it has been put down forever." He spoke with a good deal of indignation in his tones. Immediately John P. Hale rose and said, " As a member of the Free Soil party, I am very much interested in the piece of information I have just received from the Honorable Senator from Kentucky ; namely that the party to which I belong has been put ' down, down, down, so low that we never shall rise again.' I am afraid the Senator may be right. I very much fear he is correct in his statement ; since there is no

man on this floor who knows better by his own experience what it is to be put down, down, down, and
to be kept down, than the Honorable Senator from
Kentucky." Clay was hit hard by this rejoinder, he
having repeatedly lost the nomination for Presidency.
After we left the Senate chamber, I said to Hale,
" Mr. Clay will never forgive you for that speech."
" No, he never will, but what would you have ? They
may trample upon us, but they shall not trample on
us without at least hearing something in reply."

On another occasion, some one said to Hale. " The
gentleman from New Hampshire will have to eat his
words." Mr. Hale at once replied, " If I eat my words
I think I shall have a much more palatable meal
than that gentleman would have if he were to eat *his*
words."

In the year 1849, Salmon P. Chase was elected to
the Senate as a Free Soiler. The same year William
H. Seward was also elected. He was an anti-slavery
man from the first. Two years after, in 1851, Charles
Sumner was chosen to the Senate, and four years
after that, in 1855 Henry Wilson was sent as his
colleague. And thus by degrees the strength of the
anti-slavery members of the House and Senate was
much increased.

I recollect that in this winter of 1851, I used sometimes to go on Saturday evenings to the house of
Gamaliel Bailey, Editor of the " National Era." On

those evenings, anti-slavery members of Congress were wont to assemble and to meet other gentlemen of their way of thinking from different parts of the country. I met there Seward, Giddings, Chase, Hale, Julian, Slade, Horace Mann, and I think, also, John G. Palfrey. Such men were at that time unpopular in Congress ; they were in a small minority ; their influence was supposed to amount to little ; but as the wheel of time revolved they came to the summit. Seward became Secretary of State, Hale was ambassador to Russia ; Chase was Secretary of the Treasury and afterwards Chief Justice of the United States. Yet, while the power of the anti-slavery sentiment was increasing throughout the Northern States, the slave-power continued to win new triumphs.

The decision of the Supreme Court in the Prigg case, was also considered a pro-slavery triumph. Prigg seized a slave woman who had escaped into Pennsylvania. Under the laws of Pennsylvania he was arrested, indicted and sentenced to fine or imprisonment, because, by the law of that State such an arrest was not allowed. But by this decision of the Supreme Court it was settled that Congress alone had power to legislate concerning fugitives, and it was, moreover, decided that a master might seize his slave wherever he found him, and carry him out of the State without trial. As a result of this, it was assumed that if a man was claimed as a slave he must necessarily be

one. There were free northern colored people everywhere who were arrested under this ruling, and the
kidnapping of free colored people frequently took
place. They were torn from their homes and carried
off to be sold. If some brutal man wanted to make a
little money he might seize men, women or children,
carry them away and sell them, and they never would
be heard of again.

When this Prigg decision was made, some of the
people in the Northern states said, " We have been
relieved from all duty in this matter. The Courts say
we must not interfere. We will go farther, and say
we *will* not interfere." And so the legislatures
passed laws forbidding the Northern jails to receive
fugitives, and forbidding their officers to aid in the
search for them.

In 1836 Arkansas was admitted with a constitution
preventing slavery from being ever abolished, in spite
of the opposition of Adams and others.

The next triumph of the slave-power was in 1838,
when the Florida war occurred. This was occasioned
by slaveholders who had gone among the Seminoles
to recover their escaped slaves. The soldiers of our
army were employed to seize the fugitives. The
Seminoles refused to give them up. They were
pursued, and finally after a war which lasted eight
years, they were overcome, and the Seminoles were

obliged to surrender the colored fugitives, and consent
to go West themselves.

The next victory for the slave-power was in 1844,
when Mr. Samuel Hoar was sent to South Carolina
to collect information about the free colored citizens
from the North, then in prison or in slavery. When,
in obedience to a resolution of the Massachusetts
legislature Mr. Hoar went to South Carolina, there
was a great deal of excitement in Charleston, and he
was advised to return at once. He refused to go.
saying he had come to perform an important duty for
the State of Massachusetts, to find out certain facts
in regard to her citizens. The duty of the State was
to protect its citizens. He was compelled, however,
to return, as they threatened to drag him away by
force unless he went peaceably.

In December, 1843, began the agitation for the annexation of Texas. Mr. Calhoun had been Secretary
of State. The first plan, which was certainly the legal
one, was to annex it by treaty. It was urged on the
President and Senate, but it required a vote of two-
thirds of that body which they could not get. There
was immense opposition in the North, and even the
Southern States felt certain objections to this measure. It was some time before the South was united
in its favor  Th  Whig press in the South opposed
it, and the Whigs voted against it, and it was thus defeated. Mr. Clay was specially opposed to it on many

grounds.   Through the North it was understood to
be a plan of the slaveholders for getting more territory from which to carve slave states.   This immense
State of Texas, half as large as the original thirteen
states united, was to be annexed, and slavery allowed
to go into it.   Finally, by the terms by which it was
at last annexed, it was agreed that in the course of
time there should be five slave states made out of it,
adding ten slaveholders to the United States Senate.
The proposed annexation by joint resolution became
the measure on which the presidential election turned.
Polk announced himself in favor of annexation, and
Clay opposed it.   Clay was defeated and Polk elected,
and in consequence Texas was immediately annexed,
President Tyler signing the bill as acting president.
This was followed by war with Mexico.   General
Taylor was ordered by Polk to advance beyond the
Nueces, the old boundary of Texas, and this brought
on war.   Congress voted that " war existed by the
act of Mexico," although it really existed in consequence of General Taylor going into territory which
never had belonged to Texas.   This was the next
triumph of the slave-power.   By this war there was
added to the United States territory which the slave-
power thought would finally come into their possession.

About that time, in 1846, David Wilmot, a Democrat of Pennsylvania, offered a proviso to the resolu-

tion of annexation, to exclude slavery from all territory acquired from Mexico.    This was passed by a
vote of 87 to 64, but the Senate, which was intensely
Democratic, rejected the proviso in spite of the opposition of Mr. Webster and others who defended it,
and the House finally relinquished this anti-slavery
prohibition.    We then paid $15,000,000, and we ac-
quired Upper and Lower California and New Mexico.

In 1850 came the compromise measures, which
were to settle all the disputes about slavery.    Henry
Clay was the father of these measures.    The general
points included were these :—That California should
be admitted as a free state if the inhabitants so determined.    That the Wilmot proviso should *not* be applied to the territory.    That the debt of Texas should
be paid on condition of its giving up its claim to any
part of New Mexico ; and that the Fugitive Slave
Law was to be passed.    These compromises, as they
were called, occasioned a great deal of excitement.
The anti-slavery people considered that the slave-
power had won a new triumph, and felt that the whole
North was beginning to be put under the yoke of
slavery.

In 1853 and 4 came one of the measures which
startled the North more than anything else, the repeal of the Missouri compromise.    Missouri had been
received as a slave state in 1820.    It had been finally
admitted with slavery, because there was a condition

affixed that no slavery should ever after be allowed in
any territory north of 36° 30' north latitude, which
was the southern boundary of Missouri. By that
condition slavery was excluded from Kansas and Nebraska, and they were secured to freedom. Now,
having obtained their share of the bargain, the slave-
power determined to have the other part also. Stephen
A. Douglas of Illinois declared that the compromises
of 1850 had abolished the Missouri compromise, and
that slavery might now enter those states. He was
opposed by many leading men, as Chase, Sumner,
Wade, Giddings, Everett and Seward, who said it was
the violation of a sacred pledge. The debate lasted
four months, and ended in the triumph of the slave-
power, and the repeal of the Missouri restriction.

Then followed in 1854 the Kansas struggle, of
which we will speak later, together with the events
which followed. We will now return to the movement as it went on outside of Congress.

# CHAPTER III.

## ABOLITIONISTS AND THEIR ACTIVITY—FUGITIVE
## SLAVES.

" Once to every man and nation, comes the moment to decide
In the strife of Truth with Falsehood for the good or evil side.
Some great cause, God's new Messiah, offering each the bloom or
blight,
Parts the goats upon the left hand, parts the sheep upon the right."
LOWELL.

IN the last chapter I enumerated the successive
political triumphs of the slave-power in the United
States. These were as follows :—The decision of
the Supreme Court in the Prigg case, which decision
established the doctrine that the Free States had no
right to pass any laws in relation to slavery or fugitives. It was placed entirely in the power of Congress to pass any law for the recovery of fugitives,
and the Free States could not interfere to protect their
own free colored people. That was one of the first
triumphs of the slave-power. The admission of Arkansas as a slave state came in 1836 ; the Florida
war in 1838, the object of which was to secure slavery
in Georgia. In 1844 an attempt was made by Massa-

chusetts to protect her free colored seamen in Southern ports. There were many free colored people at
the North who went into the mercantile marine.
Some of the Southern states passed laws to the effect
that any colored man entering the state should be arrested and confined in jail, and at the same time pay
his expenses while there. If he did not have the
means, he was sold into slavery to pay the debt. It
was understood that free colored men from Massachusetts, sailing on her vessels, had been made slaves
in this way. and attempts were made to test the con-
stitutionality of these oppressive laws of the Southern
States. Mr. Samuel Hoar was, therefore, sent to
South Carolina by the State of Massachusetts to procure evidence and bring the cases before the United
States courts. He was, however, compelled to leave,
being driven by force out of the State. In the same
year came the annexation of Texas, followed by the
war with Mexico. The object of this was believed to
be to procure additional territory for the purposes of
slavery. It was supposed that New Mexico and California, which were obtained from Mexico, as the result of the war, would become slave states. In 1850
came what were called the compromise measures, and
the defeat of the Wilmot Proviso, which proviso was
at first supported by the majority of the Democratic
part of the House of Congress, as well as by the
Whigs. It was to the effect that any territory that

should be obtained as the result of the war should be free from slavery. This proviso was finally defeated by the slave-power. Another of these measures was the passage of the Fugitive Slave Law, by which it became much more easy for slaveholders to pursue and recover their slaves who had escaped to the other states. In consequence of this law, there were fugitives carried from Boston—a fact which had not taken place before in the memory of man. Then came, in 1853, the repeal of the Missouri Agreement, to exclude slavery north of 36° 30', so that slavery was now allowed to go into that territory, from which it had previously been shut out by mutual agreement. The Lecompton Constitution, for Kansas, followed in 1857, which was a Pro-slavery Constitution, making Kansas a slave state, and one which was passed in opposition to a majority of the actual inhabitants by the power of Missourians, who invaded the State for that purpose.

These Missouri slaveholders crowded across the state line to Kansas, and took possession of the polls. In 1856, came the attack on Charles Sumner by Preston Brooks, in consequence of his speech on the wrongs of the people of Kansas. He was struck down by violent blows of a cudgel while in his seat in the Senate Chamber, and was so disabled that he could not return for four years. Brooks resigned his seat, knowing that he might be expelled, but was im-

mediately re-elected to Congress, and through his act
he became a hero.   There was scarcely any press, or
public man in the South, who did not boldly declare
that he had done right.   In 1857, came the Dred
Scott Decision.   This decision delivered by a majority of the judges of the Supreme Court of the
United States, including Chief Justice Taney, and
read by him, decided that the colored people in the
United States were not citizens ; that no colored man
could become a citizen ; and that he had no rights before the law.   In this decision, Judge Taney made the
well-known and often-quoted statement,that at the time
of the adoption of the Constitution, it was considered
that " the colored man had no rights which the white
man was bound to respect."   This statement was
made in apparent forgetfulness of all that had been
said by Washington and others concerning the rights
of all men.   Before that time the South had only
claimed, that if a slave escaped to a free state, the
slaveholder had a right to take him.   It was now decided, that if the slaveholder himself took him into a
free state, and he escaped, the holder had a right to
recover him.

There were able and conclusive arguments read by
Justices McClean and Curtis in opposition to this decision.   Those of us who had long known Benjamin
R. Curtis, and his great ability, were proud of the
commanding power with which he gave his dissent

from the decision of Judge Taney. But his arguments were overborne by the majority of the Court.

All these aggressions and successes of the slave-power were new fuel to the fire of the anti-slavery agitation. They supplied fresh and convincing arguments for the Northern agitators. Everything that the slaveholders did prevented the anti-slavery meetings from becoming commonplace. Every one of these gatherings offered some new grounds for showing the evils of slavery, and the wrongs done by the slave-power to the North. In innumerable meetings held at the North these wrongs were described and exposed ; and, I suppose when we come to look back on it, we shall say there never was a people educated so thoroughly in so short a time, as the voters of the North were, to see the evil, the wrongs and dangers of slavery. Perpetual agitation went forward, by the activity and zeal of the anti-slavery orators and writers. They published papers and tracts, held conventions, and took every opportunity to keep this subject before the people. For instance, on the first of August, the anniversary of emancipation in the West Indies, they would hold conventions all over the country. Always, too, these were held on the Fourth of July, when they would read the famous introductory sentence to the Declaration of Independence. " We hold these truths to be self-evident, that all men are created equal, and endowed by their Creator with inalienable rights, among which are life, liberty, and the pursuit of happiness." Mr. Emerson once said, " Eloquence is dog-cheap in anti-slavery meetings." At another time he spoke of the " enraged eloquence" of Faneuil Hall. Some one said of Luther, that his words were half battles. So we might say of these meetings, that each one was half a battle. The anti-slavery men welcomed contradiction, and rejoiced in the opportunity of meeting an opponent. If any slaveholder was known to be in Boston, he was invited to come upon the platform and state his views ; and there were always plenty of people to answer him. Garrison and his friends were always ready—always prepared with facts and arguments ; and the opponent whom the Lord delivered into their hands was usually much to be pitied.

Sometimes a man would innocently beseech them to be mild and calm in their treatment of slaveholders. The answer to this would be, " Suppose, sir, *your* wife and child were taken from you, and sent to Albamba to be the slaves of any brute who had money enough to buy them, would *you* be calm then ? Would you speak gently, and say that in your opinion this was an unwise course, and not altogether desirable ? We are arguing the cause of thousands of husbands and fathers, liable at any moment to have their families torn from them. To be calm in such a cause would be a sin." Sometimes a Southerner would come forward, declaring the slaves happy, well-treated and contented. Immediately the anti-slavery orators would read numerous advertisements in Southern papers, offering rewards for runaway slaves, alive or dead, who were described as marked with stripes, and mutilated, showing the ill-treatment they had endured. " If they are so happy, why do they run away ? If so contented and well-behaved, why are they beaten, and shot, and mutilated ? "

" The "timid good" might stand aloof from these meetings, but the mob was present, and there was sure to be a crowd, either of friends or foes, and always something worth hearing. There was often disorder and tumult, but the anti-slavery speakers on the platform were perfctly calm. Some of them seemed to be like the warhorse in the Book of Job, that " scented the battle from afar—the tumult and the shouting." These men delighted in the fury of this battle. I remember on one occasion there was an anti-slavery meeting where everything seemed to be quiet and peaceful, and the orators were listened to with much attention. Then Stephen Foster suddenly rose and said : " We are not doing our duty. If we were doing our duty this audience, instead of listening to us so quietly, would be throwing brick-bats at us." Charles Burleigh, in the middle of his speech once, had a rotten egg thrown at him, which struck him in the face. With ready wit, as he calm-

ly wiped his face, he said, " I have always maintained
that pro-slavery arguments are very unsound." There
were some quite rude jokes made, and a good deal of
fun—fun made of the abolitionists as well as of their
opponents. They could enjoy a good joke even at
their own expense. Mr. Garrison was nearly bald.
Charles C. Burleigh had a very long beard, which
came almost down to his waist. Once in the midst
of a most earnest discussion, some wag cried out,
" Burleigh ! why don't you cut off your beard and
give it to Garrison to make a wig of ? " This, of
course, caused a great deal of fun. On the platform
you would always see Garrison ; with him was my
classmate and friend, Sam May. Stephen S. Foster
was always there. Sometimes Mr. Sam E. Sewell
was to be seen, who was one of the earliest to join
this party. He was with Garrison at the first meeting, and is still living in an honored old age. There,
too, one saw in the early days William W. White, (a
brother of Maria White Lowell,) who died too soon.
He was a very brilliant man, and always made very
admirable speeches. Parker Pilsbury, James Buffum,
Arnold Buffum, Elizur Wright, Henry C. Wright,
Abigail Kelley, Lucy Stone, Theo. D. Weld, the sisters Grimké, from South Carolina ; John T. Sargent,
Mrs. Chapman, Mrs. Lydia M. Child, Fred Douglas,
Wm. W. Brown and Francis Jackson. The last was
a stern Puritan, conscientious, upright, clear-minded,

universally respected. Edmund Quincy also was there, and he never spoke without saying something that had a touch of wit as well as of logic. Oliver Johnson is still living, and he was one of the very first members of the Society. Theodore Parker, Samuel J. May, John Pierpont, Chas. L. Stearns, Chas. L. Redmond, Geo. Thompson (another wonderfully eloquent man), and, above all Wendell Phillips.

I have no doubt I have omitted some whom I ought to remember, but this list shows what men and women met on the Garrison platform to argue this cause. All were intrepid, clear-headed, ready to meet and answer any opponent, and delighted if they could get an opponent on the platform to answer. There was no such excitement to be had anywhere else as at these meetings. There was a little of everything going on in them. Sometimes crazy people would come in and insist on taking up the time ; sometimes mobs would interrupt the smooth tenor of their way ; but amid all disturbance each meeting gave us an interesting and impressive hour. I think that some of the Garrisonian orators had the keenest tongues ever given to man. Stephen S. Foster and Henry C. Wright, for example, said the sharpest things that were ever uttered. Their belief was that people were asleep, and the only thing to be done was to rouse them ; and to do this it was necessary to cut deep and not to spare for their crying. The more angry people were made the better it was for them. The titles of some of their tracts indicate this purpose. Pilsbury wrote one called " The Church the Forlorn Hope of Slavery ; " Foster another called " The Church the Brotherhood of Thieves."

Some pursued a different course. Among these must be especially named Samuel J. May, a man who united in a remarkable degree perfect courage with entire kindliness. He was a singular example of the way in which truth can be spoken in love. It was almost impossible to resist such a fine union of gentleness and strength. The motto of his life might have been the words which I once saw upon the great organ in the cathedral at Pisa : " Out of the strong cometh forth sweetness." *

I recollect Mr. May's once giving me an account of a conversation he had with a Southerner at the house of Henry Colman, in Deerfield, where he was to pass the night. Mr. May arrived just before sundown, after having spent the day at an anti-slavery meeting. Mr. Colman met him at the door and said, " My dear Mr. May, I hope you will say nothing on the subject of slavery this evening, for we have a Southern gentleman here who is very excitable and irritable, and it would be quite unpleasant to have a discussion. Mr.

* See an interesting volume, written by Mr. May, called "Some Recollections of the Anti-Slavery Conflict," Boston, 1809 ; also ; " Life of S. J. May," by Thomas Mumford.

May replied, " I will not introduce the subject, but if
I am asked any questions I shall be obliged to answer
them according to the truth." He was introduced to
this Southerner, and sat down beside him in the room.
On the other side of the Southerner was a lady who
had heard that Mr. May had been to the anti-slavery
meeting ; and, leaning forward in front of the Southerner she asked, " What did you do at the anti-sla.
ery meeting to-day ? " Thereupon Mr. May proceeded
to give her an account of it, so arranging what he
said as to convey to this Southern gentleman an idea
of what was the real purpose of the anti-slavery people. He spoke in such a way as to disabuse him of
the notion that they had any intention of exciting an
insurrection among the slaves. Their appeal was to
the reason and conscience of the slaveholder, and the
things of which they were often accused were far
from their thought. He observed that this man became interested and excited, and finally turning to
him " Mr. May," he said, " I should like to know what
business you have with this thing at all ? What business is it of yours, sir ? It is our own affair altogether.
You people here at the North have nothing to do with
it." " But my dear sir," answered Mr. May, very
mildly, " you do not believe, certainly, that slavery is
right ? " " No, I don't think it is right in the ab-
stract ; but you don't know anything about it. You
are doing mischief and making trouble by all you try

to do." Thereupon Mr. May proceeded to argue with him in his gentle, but strong manner, and finally after they had been talking for half an hour or more, this Southerner began to walk up and down the room with a great deal of excitement. At last he turned and said to Mr. May, " You must not think as badly of us as if we had been brought up at the North and had the opportunity of hearing these arguments year after year." " Oh, no," said Mr. May, " I cannot think so badly of you, considering the influences you have been under all your lives. I think it is not unnatural that you should feel as you do. But I do think this, that we at the North, who have always enjoyed the blessings of a free State, ought to take every opportunity in our power of doing all we can to bring this evil system to an end. I should think very badly of myself if I did not do so."

Mr. May, while in Syracuse was one of the managers of the underground railroad, the object of which was to enable the slaves to escape. It helped only those who wanted to escape ; those who were dissatisfied with their condition, and who were willing to encounter the risks of getting away. There were anti-slavery people all the way along the route—people willing to protect these fugitives and send them on to the next station, where they would be protected. Before a great while had passed, this became so well organized a system, that these station masters knew just where to send the slaves from their own house to the next station on the road. The system extended from Kentucky and Virginia across Ohio ; from Maryland through Pennsylvania, and New York to New England and Canada.

There were many people in the slave states, even slaveholders, who were willing to secrete fugitives if paid enough for doing it. This I learned from a colored woman who was famous for having got off many fugitives from the South. She had helped so many hundred to escape that they called her "Moses." She once passed an evening at my house, and gave us an account of her methods. She said she first obtained enough money, then went to Maryland, where she privately collected a party of slaves and got them ready to start. She first satisfied herself that they had enough courage and firmness to run the risks. She next made arrangements so that they should set out on Saturday night, as there would be no opportunity on Sunday for advertising them, so that they had that day's start on their way north. Then she had places prepared where she knew she could be sure that they could be protected and taken care of if she had the money to pay for that protection. When she was at the North she tried to raise funds until she got a certain amount, and then went south to carry out this plan. She always paid some colored man to follow after the person who put up the posters advertising

the runaways, and pull them down as fast as they were
put up, so that about five minutes after each was up
it was taken away. She seemed to have indomitable
courage herself, and a great deal of prudence. She
told me that once when in Baltimore, she found a
negro cook, a woman who had suffered very much,
who had had her children taken from her and sold,
and who was determined to escape. She wanted
Moses to help her. Moses replied, "If you are willing
to come with me I will take you across to Delaware."
So they went upon a steamer which was to sail from
Baltimore to Delaware. When they were aboard she
told the woman to stay in one part of the boat, by one
of the outside guards, and she herself went to the
clerk and asked for two tickets to the place she wished
to go. He looked at her and said, "I do not know
whether we can let you have them. You will have to
wait a little while." She went back very much alarmed.
She knew that if there was any investigation made it
would be found that this woman was a slave, and she
would be seized. She went and sat down by the side
of the woman, and the woman said, softly, "Have you
got the tickets?" Moses made no reply. "I looked
straight at the water," said she, "and a great darkness
came over me. All at once everything brightened
again and I saw a great light which glowed all over
the river. 'Yes, I have got them now, I am sure of
it,' I replied." After a little while the clerk came to

her and said, "Here, Aunty, are your tickets," and she succeeded in escaping with the woman through Delaware to New Jersey.

In Boston there were many places where fugitives were received and taken care of. Every anti-slavery man was ready to protect them, and among these were some families not known to be anti-slavery. My neighbor and friend, Mr. George S. Hillard, was an United States commissioner. It might be his business after the slave law was passed to issue a warrant to the marshal for the capture of slaves. But Mrs. Hillard, his wife, was in the habit of putting the fugitives in the upper chamber of their own house, and I think Mr. Hillard was aware of the fact and never interfered. There was once a colored man, a fugitive, put in this upper room, and when Mrs. Hillard went in she found he had carefully pulled down the shades of the window. She told him she did not think there was any danger of his being seen from the street. "Perhaps not, Missis," he replied, "but I do not want to spoil the place." He knew that after he had gone, there would come some one else who would need to be protected. He did not want any one to see his colored face there, lest it might excite suspicion, to the injury of his successors.

Most persons have heard the story of William and Ellen Crafts. Ellen Crafts was a very light mulatto woman who would easily pass for white. She was

nurse in a family in South Carolina, and did not think
of escaping. She was married to a man, darker than
herself. But on one occasion her mistress intended
to go North, and wanted to take this colored nurse.
Ellen Crafts had a little babe of her own. She was
expecting to take her infant with her, till her mistress
said, " You don't think that I am going to have that
child with me. No, indeed." So the little babe was left
behind and died during its mother's absence. When
Ellen got home she made up her mind to escape. It
took her a good while to make her plans. At last she
determined to disguise herself as a young Southern
gentleman and take her husband as a body servant.
In order that it might not be seen that she had no
beard she professed to have great suffering from her
teeth, and had a poultice put round her face. In order
that she might not be asked to write she had her right
arm in a sling, as though an injury had befallen it·
So they got off together one morning. They reached
Baltimore safely, although she noticed in the train a
gentleman who had often seen her at her master's
house. When she got to Baltimore she had to meet
the difficulty of getting out of a slave state into a free
one, for which a special pass for her servant was
necessary. She had none, of course, but she assumed
the haughty airs of a Southerner, and when they declined to give her a ticket for her servant, she said,
" Why, what can I do. You see my arm ; you see my

face in this condition! I *must* have him to take care of me." So by dint of perseverance she succeeded, and they arrived finally in Boston. The master of William Crafts heard that he was in Boston, and sent on papers to have him arrested under the fugitive slave law. It was understood that he was to be arrested, and he was prepared to defend himself. He said he would kill the United States marshal if he attempted to arrest him. But some of his friends told him that this would be a very bad thing for his race, and would only make their condition worse. Then it was arranged that he should be taken to the house of Ellis Gray Loring at Brookline, Mass. Mr. Loring happened to be away, and the honorable nature of Crafts was seen when he found that Mr. Loring was not at home. He asked to see Mrs Loring, and said to her, "I cannot stay when your husband is away." "Oh," said Mrs. Loring, "nothing would suit him better than to have you stay." "That may be so," said Crafts, "but he does not know that I am here, and if anything bad happens to you or to him, I shall feel that I have done very wrong." It was with difficulty that he was at last persuaded by Mrs. Loring to remain.

There were a great many people who could never be made to believe that it was right to return a fugitive. If a man had the courage, determination and love of liberty which would enable him to encoun-

ter the dangers of escaping, they thought it was the
height of meanness to send him back.   Even some
Southerners took that view.   I recollect when I lived
in Kentucky, there was a friend of mine, Mr, Goodwin from Plymouth, who had hired a little girl named
Milly.   She had grown up with him and his wife, and
Mrs. Goodwin had taught her to read and write, to sew,
and given her a knowledge of housekeeping.   She was
at that time seventeen or eighteen years old.   The
owner of the girl was an English gentleman, named
Booth, who had lived in Kentucky for many years.   I
was sitting in Mr. Goodwin's office one day with Mr.
Booth, when a letter came to Mr. Goodwin from his
wife, in which was enclosed a letter to herself from
Milly.   Milly said that she had decided to go away
to a free state.   Mr. Goodwin read aloud Milly's
letter : " It breaks my heart," said the letter, " to leave
you, my dear mistress.   I shall never find so good a
friend in the world as you have been to me, never any
one that I shall love so much.   But you have taught
me many things, and among them the value of freedom.   All the education you have given me has gone
to make me feel that I have no right to remain a
slave when I can be free.   I am obliged to leave you.
I hope I may some time see you again, but I do not
know.   I want you to know how grateful I am and
always shall be for all your kindness."

While this letter was being read aloud I watched

the face of the owner of this girl. It was a hard face
and I could not tell what he was thinking or feeling.
This was a loss to him of from $1,500 to $2,000.
When the letter was through he turned to me and
said, " Mr. Clarke, if you or I had been in the girl's
place we should have done the same thing. I do not
blame her. I shall not try to get her back." That
is the way honorable men at the South felt in those
days.

I recollect, after Burns had been arrested in Boston,
and taken south, I met Marshal Barnes, formerly
United States Marshal, under a Democratic adminis-
tration, and he said to me, " Friend Devens has made
a mistake." " How so ? " said I, " When I was a
marshal, and they tried to make me find their slaves,
I would say, ' I don't know where your niggers are,
but I will see if I can find out.' So I always went to
Garrison's office and said, ' I want you to find such
and such a negro ; tell me where he is.' The next
thing I knew, the fellow would be in Canada."
But it is true, as Marshal Barnes said, that Judge
Devens made a mistake, he did it honestly. and with
an honorable purpose. He thought, when he had
taken the oath of United States Marshal, he ought
not to shrink from the duties of the office. He made
a noble atonement for this error, if error it was. Before he went to the war, he called on Mrs. Lydia
Maria Child, and told her that he was in negotiation

with the owner of Burns to have him ransomed and
brought north, and made free. The negotiation was
not quite complete, and he would deposit $1,800 with
Mrs. Child to settle the thing ; which she did. Burns
thus became a free man, General Devens having paid
the full amount to his master.

One of the most interesting stories of the fugitives,
was that of a man called Father Henson, who has
just died at the age of ninety-five years. He was
often in Boston, and was much esteemed and liked by
all who knew him. He was brought up as a slave in
Virginia. He grew to be a young man without ever
hearing a sermon. The first one he heard, at a camp-
meeting converted him, and made of him a religious
man. That single sermon did· more for him than a
great many for the most of us. On his way home
from the meeting, the sense of God's presence, and
his own needs, came over him with such power, that
he knelt down in a corner of the fence and prayed.
Then light and peace came to him, and he rose a new
man. He was entirely trusted by his master, who,
having got into some pecuniary trouble, and being
afraid that the sheriff would come and attach the
slaves on his plantation, called Henson and said to
him, " I am going to trust you with something which
is very important. You know I have a brother in
Kentucky. I am going to send my slaves to Kentucky under your care. I will give you this money to

use by the way." Henson took these twenty or thirty
slaves through Virginia, to the Ohio river, and there
bought a flat boat and went down the river. He
stopped at Cincinnati, where, if he had chosen, he
could have escaped with all of them, but he felt that
he had been trusted, and must fulfil the trust. When
he told me this, he said, " If the Lord will forgive me
for not setting them free, and I ever have another
opportunity, I am quite sure I shall do better than
that." He took the slaves on to Kentucky, and there
delivered them over to the Kentucky master, and
there they remained. After a while some of them
were sold to the South to pay the debts of the Virginia
master. Henson being a kind of Methodist preacher,
was sometimes allowed to go away and preach, and
after preaching he would take up a little collection.
This he would lay by'to purchase freedom. At last
he went to his master in Virginia, to see if he could
buy his liberty. At first the owner refused his consent,
but his son said, " Father ! remember all Henson has
done ; you ought to let him pay for his freedom." The
master finally consented, or pretended to consent. He
took the money, and gave him his free papers, and
Henson set out to return to Kentucky. On his way
down the river the boat came opposite to the plantation ; but instead of landing at his master's house, he
went ashore near his own cabin. When he got there
his wife said, " There is news about you." " What is

it ? " " Some of the servants overheard them talking in the big house. Master said that you thought you had bought yourself, but that he was going to take your papers and keep them, and you would not be free till you had paid a good deal more." Henson said, " That is too bad. Wife, look here ! I did have my papers ! I had them when I was in Cincinnati. I saw them there in my bag. If you find them there, do what you please with them." She took the papers and put them between two slabs of board, and buried them. The next morning he went to the master's house, when the horn sounded to call the servants to work. The master called out. " You have got back, have you, Henson ? What did you do ? Have you got your free papers ? " " Oh, master, I had them when I was in Cincinnati. I saw them in my bag there." " What ! lost them ? Where did you get off ? " " I landed near my cabin, and walked through the woods to it." " You must have lost them on the way. Go back and see if you can find them." " Do you think so, master, I'll go and look. So he went back and pretended to search diligently for the papers ; but, naturally, he did not see them anywhere. The next thing that happened was that the master determined to send him down the river with his son, taking charge of a flatboat loaded with bacon and corn. The understanding was, that after the cargo and the flatboat were sold, Henson was to be sold in New

Orleans, away from wife and children and home. That came to his knowledge, and made him almost crazy.

On the way down the river, he and his young master being alone—his master being asleep—he sat and thought of all the wrongs he had suffered ; and how hard after all he had done, that he should be so treated. He could bear it no longer. He took the axe in his hand, intending to kill his young master. As he approached the place, he seemed to hear a voice saying, " Henson, will you throw it all away? will you throw it all away ? " and he understood that some voice from Heaven was asking him if he would throw away all the good he had tried to do, by this act of violence. He threw the axe aside, and went back to his place, and said, " I leave it all to you, Lord ; let it be done as you will ; I leave it all to you." When they reached New Orleans, and the cargo had been sold, it so chanced, or it came by Providence, that the young man was taken ill with yellow fever ; and when he was well enough to go North, he said, " You must go back with me, Henson ; I must have you as a nurse." So he went back to Kentucky. When he reached home he said to his wife, " Now, wife, you must do as you think best, but as for me, I am bound for freedom." His wife said she would go, too ; and as they had some small children, it was arranged that they should have a bag made big enough to hold the two children. He had, also, some stilts made in order to escape the scent of bloodhounds. He practised every night walking on the stilts and carrying the little children. When the time came for going, they all went up the big chimney of the cabin to the roof, got on their stilts and walked away, carrying the little ones in the bag, until they reached a stream. They went down the brook to the river, crossed it in a skiff that he had prepared, and in that way they escaped.

These fugitives stories produced a great effect on all who heard them. It was impossible to convince the people that it was right to send back to slavery men who were so desirous of freedom as to run such risks. All our education, from boyhood up to manhood, had taught us to believe that it was the duty of all men to struggle for freedom. " Give me liberty, or give me death." These men took their lives in their hands. They were pursued by bloodhounds, exposed to famine. They were frozen and starved while hiding in the swamps. If caught, they were subjected to most severe punishments. They dared it all, and finally, if some of them escaped. ought they to be sent back again ? The human conscience, reason, and heart, all said " No,"

I was once, with my wife, in Columbus, Ohio, and having a day to spare, we employed it in visiting the public institutions. Among other places we went to the Penitentiary, and were introduced by the warden to a colored man who had escaped from Alabama. He had taken a whole year in coming from Alabama to Cincinnati. He had travelled only in the night, hiding in the woods during the day. He had nothing to eat but what he could get from the fields, sometimes finding a chicken, green corn, or perhaps a small pig. At last he reached Cincinnati. Then he thought he was in a free city, and that he was safe. He went around to get something to do, and was told by a man who had a horse to sell that he would give him ten dollars to sell it. It was a stolen horse. The poor fellow was arrested as a thief, and sent to the penitentiary. The warden told me he had no doubt the man's story was true, and it was his intention to get him pardoned by the Governor. Meantime the lawyer who had undertaken to defend him, had written to the colored man once or twice that he should try for a pardon; but the warden feared it was the object of this lawyer to turn the fugitive over to his master, and so obtain a reward. "But," said the warden, "I shall not allow him to do so. When the time comes for the Governor to pardon him, he will go at once to Canada." A month after this we were in Buffalo, at a hotel. A waiter came behind my chair and asked if he could see us in our room. It proved to be this man. I asked him why he was not in Canada. He said he had been to Canada, but there was so little means of getting a support there that he had decided

to come to Buffalo, and as soon as he got enough to
buy a small farm he would go back.

There was one fugitive called " Box Brown," because he had himself packed up in a wooden box and
was brought thus from Virginia to Pennsylvania.

Another man, Edward Davis, escaped under the
guards of a steamer which left Charleston for Philadelphia. H  remained under the guards during a
large part of the night until he was nearly drowned.
Finding he could endu. it no longer, he called out to
the sailors. On reaching Philadelphia he was turned
over to the police and sent back to slavery.

Mr. May, in his " Recollections," has given an account of the fugitives who often were in his house in
Syracuse, N. Y. They came from all the Southern
States, and arrived at all hours of the night. They
were often very dirty and squalid ; but to be received
by that benign and kindly friend, whose very look was
a benediction, must have been like entering Heaven.
He tells of one man who refused to enter the house,
saying, "O, Massa, not fit." " No," answered the
philanthropist, " you are pot now, but soon shall be."
So taking into the barn a tub of warm water, soap,
towels, and a suit of clothes, he made him wash himself thoroughly, throw all his clothes on the dunghill,
and dress in the suit of clean clothes. Another
young colored man arrived well-dressed, and with a
soft hand. He had been employed to drive his mis-

tress and daughters, and wait on the table. He had been treated kindly, and taught to read by his young mistress ; but he learned that he was to be sold, and so ran away. Another day there came a well-dressed young lady, of so light a color that she could pass for white. She had been employed as chambermaid on a boat, and had laid up money given her in presents, but was about to be sold, and so she escaped in an English ship to New York, and was forwarded from there to Syracuse by the underground road, and was then sent by Mr. May to Canada.

When those who helped fugitives were asked why they did so, they referred to cases in history to show that it had always been considered a duty to shelter fugitives. There was the story in Herodotus of the message sent by the Athenians to the oracle at Delphos, to ask if they should protect fugitives from the great king even at the risk of war. The oracle said, "No! send them back." The messengers, seeing that birds had built their nests in the temple, began to pull them down. The priestess asked why they disturbed these suppliants. " Because you tell us to send away our suppliants." " I did so," answered the oracle, " but it was because you have offended me, and I wished you to suffer the penalty which the Gods will inflict on you, if you refuse to protect your suppliants." So, too, there was the story of Sir John Jervis, Lord St. Vincent, who was asked by a bio-

grapher what he considered the chief exploit of his
life. " I was once," he answered, " lying in the harbor of Algiers, and two slaves swam from the shore
and came on board. The Dey of Algiers demanded
their surrender. I refused. He threatened to order
his forts to fire on my vessel. I replied that on the
first shot fired, I would place my ship abreast of the
fort and blow it to atoms. I heard no more of the
matter." This action pleased the great naval com-
mander more than the victory which brought him his
earldom.

Those who defended slavery were accustomed to
speak of the free colored people as idle, as beggars
and criminals. But this was a libel. You seldom
saw a colored person begging in the Northern cities,
and the criminal statistics showed that in proportion
to their numbers few were committed to the prisons.
In Cincinnati, in 1851, there were many colored people who possessed a considerable amount of property.
One of the best hotels, the Dumas House, was owned
and managed by colored people. One of them had
the best shop for family groceries. Another was the
best photographer. So it probably was in other cities.
I, however, know that this was the case in Cincinnati, having spent some days in investigating the condition of the colored people in 1851. I recollect asking about their habits of temperance, and was told
that at one time nearly all the colored people of Cin-

cinnati belonged to the Temperance Society, having been induced to join it by the generous and devoted labors among them of Theodore D. Weld, a Divinity Student in Lane Seminary.

## CHAPTER IV.

### FRIENDS AND OPPOSERS IN THE FREE-STATES, OF THE ANTI-SLAVERY MOVEMENT.

" New occasions teach new duties. Time makes ancient good un-
couth,
They must upward still and onward who would keep abreast with
Truth.
Lo! before us gleam her camp-fires! we ourselves must Pilgrims be,
Launch our Mayflower, and steer boldly through the desperate winter
sea."

LOWELL.

THE subject of this chapter is the friends of the
anti-slavery movement and its opposers. We will
begin with those who opposed it. In the former
chapter I mentioned how many influences were combined to resist anti-slavery. Some of these were
natural and inevitable. There was the natural conservatism of age ; there was the fear of change ; the
dread of danger to the Union ; the conviction that we
had made a contract with the South, and had no right
to violate our contract. From such considerations as
these, and from the belief that the anti-slavery men
were mad fanatics, who cared not what means they
used to attain their end, there were found in the

North many very respectable, kind-hearted and conscientious people, resisting for a long time the anti-slavery movement.   Dr. Channing found fault with the bitterness and violence of the Garrison party. When Mr. Garrison declared the Constitution of the United States " a covenant with death and an agreement with hell," when Wendell Phillips uttered his " curse on the Constitution," when the Church was called " a brotherhood of thieves," it was natural enough for those who looked from the outside to think the movement a fanaticism.   Yet on the other hand, how natural it was for the abolitionists to use any language, and seize any weapon which would rouse a generation asleep over the awful iniquities and dangers of this evil system.   They had to cry aloud and spare not.   If they called the indifferent and hostile community " a generation of vipers," John the Baptist had done the same.   The gentle Jesus called the Pharisees, " Hypocrites," " blind guides," " children of hell," " tombs fair on the outside but inwardly full of dead men's bones," " serpents," " generation of vipers."   No one can understand the terrible severity of the abolitionists, who does not know what the horrors of slavery were, with which, however, they had become more familiar than the slaveholders themselves.   I recollect reading for the first time, in Kentucky, Theodore D. Weld's " American Slavery as it is ; or, Testimony of a Thousand Witnesses ; " and I still feel the sickening sensation of suffering which it caused me. It was long before I could get over the fearful impression. Another work was Frederick Law Olmstead's travels through the Southwestern States, containing a description of the way in which the slaves were treated. Other books were, " The Fugitive Slave Law and its Victims," a tract published by the · Anti-Slavery Society. " The New Reign of Terror," and Stroud's " Laws of Slavery," which last showed slavery not as it was practised by cruel and brutal masters, but as the laws of the Slave States made it.

I give a few extracts from this work, the authenticity of which was never questioned:—

" Every assemblage of negroes for the purpose of religious worship, when such worship is conducted by a negro, shall be an unlawful assembly, and a justice may issue his warrant to an officer or other person, requiring him to enter any place where such assemblage may be, and seize any negro therein, and he or any other justice may order such negro to be punished with stripes."—Code of Virgina, 1849.

By the laws of several of the slaveholding States manumitted and other free persons of color, however respectable their character, might be arrested when in the prosecution of lawful business, and if documentary evidence of their right to freedom could not be produced by them, they were thrust into prison by

law, and advertised and sold as runaway slaves.
(Laws of Maryland and Mississippi). "If a slave was
found beyond the limits of the town in which he lived,
or off the plantation where he was usually employed,
without the company of a white person, or without
the written permission of his master or employer, any
person might apprehend and punish him with a whip
on the bare back, and if he should assail and strike
such white person, he might be lawfully killed."—
(Laws of South Carolina, Brevard's Digest).

Or you may read if you please the description of
slavery on her husband's plantation, given by Mrs.
Frances Anne Kemble : or you may read the stories
told by the fugitives in the " Life of Isaac T. Hopper."
Even now, when it is all over, the flesh creeps, and
the blood curdles in the veins, at the account of the
dreadful cruelties practised on the slaves in many
parts of the South. I would advise no one to read
such histories to-day unless his nerves are very well
strung. What was it then when the stories were told
by the fugitives themselves ? What was it when the
cries of the sufferers were going up every hour ?
When the slaveholders were adding new territory to
defile with blood ? Under such conditions you could
hardly expect from those who knew these facts, mod-
erate language and soft words. The anti-slavery
men were like a cannon ball which flies straight to its
mark and shatters everything in its way. They were

terribly in earnest, and like Luther, every one of their
words was half a battle.

Let me give a few examples of the fanaticism of
the other side ; of the bitterness and narrowness
of the opposition to the abolitionists in the Northern
States.

Take the case of Miss Prudence Crandall, a respectable white lady, and a member of the Society of
Friends. In 1832, she opened a school for girls in
Canterbury, Conn. A colored girl applied for admission to the school ; there was a violent opposition to
her admission, and when Miss Crandall refused to dis
miss her, the white girls left. It was then made a
school for colored girls. Miss Crandall then became
the object of insult and persecution from her neigh-
bors, and they tried to expel her by law from the town.

Failing in this, they had a law passed by the Legislature, that no school for colored people should be
opened in the State, to which any colored pupils from
outside of the State should come. Miss Crandall was
arrested and put into jail because she was willing to
help educate respectable and well-behaved colored
girls. Mr. Samuel J May, who lived in an adjacent
town, defended her in her loneliness, and stood by her
through it all. Arthur Tappan, of New York, sent
money to secure counsel for her. After she was released on bail, the people continued to molest her.
Even the physician refused to visit her house when

there was sickness there. The trustees of the church in the town refused to let her bring her children to the house of God. When she was tried they did not succeed in convicting her, but so much violence was threatened, and so much terror was caused to the young girls in her family, that, by the advice of her friends, she closed her school and sent home the children. And all this happened, not in the slave States, but in New England, among the descendants of the Puritans. In 1836, Edward Everett, Governor of Massachusetts, an eminent scholar and a true patriot, as was afterward shown in the civil war, sent a message to the Legislature suggesting that some legislative action should be taken to prevent the anti-slavery agitation in Massachusetts, when calculated to stir up agitation in the South. The members of the Anti-Slavery Society asked to be heard before a committee, to which this part of the message was referred. They had a hearing, and Mr. George Lunt, of Newburyport, was chairman of the committee, and the meeting was addressed by Mr. Samuel J. May, Ellis Gray Loring, Garrison, and Professor Charles Follen. The last was a scholar and friend of liberty, who was exiled from Germany because an advocate of the freedom of the people there. In his argument he suggested that if any law was passed by the Legislature which seemed to be aimed at the Anti-Slavery Society, there would be danger that it might produce mobs. As soon as he said this, Mr. Lunt ordered him to sit down, and said that such suggestions were disrespectful to the committee, and refused to allow Doctor Follen to proceed. The anti-slavery men applied for another hearing to the Legislature, and Samuel E. Sewall, Dr. Follen and Wm. Goodell spoke again. Both were again interrupted by Mr. Lunt. Mr. George Bond, an eminent merchant, universally respected, arose and protested against the course taken by Mr. Lunt, who replied to him in the same insolent tone as to the other gentlemen. Mr. Lunt has recently questioned the truth of the description of his overbearing conduct as given in Wilson's History and in Samuel J. May's " Recollections ; " but the evidence of this conduct is full and positive.*

On this occasion an incident occurred which is mentioned by Harriet Martineau, and printed in an article in the Westminster Review, called the " Martyr Age in America." She says that while this discussion was going on, the door of the room opened, and Dr. William E. Channing appeared. He was very much of an invalid. It was a harsh day, and he did not go out much in the winter. He stood a moment in the doorway, wrapped in his cloak. As soon as he

---

* The account of Mr. Lunt's behavior is given in full in Samuel J. May's " Recollections," and " Wilson's Rise and Fall of the Slave-Power," and I have letters from Samuel E. Sewall and Charles K. Whipple, who were both present, and who assure me that the account in Wilson is not at all exaggerated.

was seen, several gentlemen stepped forward and offered him a seat, but without taking it, he looked around until he saw where Mr. Garrison was sitting, and went and sat down by his side. The striking thing about this action was, that Dr. Channing and Mr. Garrison did not agree about the mode of putting an end to slavery. They had differed on this matter and Mr. Garrison had spoken with considerable sharpness of Dr. Channing and his course. But on this occasion Dr. Channing meant to have it seen that he was in full sympathy with Mr. Garrison's purposes, and who wholly opposed to any attempt to stifle free discussion iin Massachusetts. The next event which occurred was the Alton mob and the murder of Lovejoy. The city of Alton, opposite St. Louis, was at that time a growing place, and Mr. Elijah P. Lovejoy the editor of an orthodox newspaper in St. Louis, opposed to slavery, but also opposed to Mr. Garrison and immediate emancipation. But because he was opposed to slavery he was driven from St. Louis. He went to Alton and established his newspaper there. His press was destroyed by a mob; he obtained a second and third, and the mob destroyed them also. He then procured a *fourth* press, and had forty armed men ready to protect it as it was brought from the steamer into a stone building. It was thought that it would be safe there, and most of the defenders went away. After the night came on, Lovejoy and a few

friends remained to protect the press and the building. A large mob collected; they fired at the windows
and the defenders returned the fire, and one man on
the outside was killed. The Mayor tried in vain to
repress the mob. Finally they put ladders to the
roof and set fire to it. Mr Lovejoy came out with his
men and looked for the assailants ; one man fired at him
from behind a pile of boards and killed him.    When
this news came to Boston, Dr. Channing and others
applied for the use of Faneuil Hall to protest against
such mob violence.  It was refused.  Dr. Channing
then appealed to the citizens of Boston, asking, " Has
Boston fallen so low that its citizens cannot be trusted
to come together to defend the principles of liberty
for which their fathers died ?   Are our fellow-citizens
to be murdered in defending their rights, and are we
not to be allowed to express our abhorrence of the
deed ? "   In response to this address a public meeting
was called in another place ; George Bond was the
chairman, and Benjamin F. Hallett the secretary.
They again applied for the use of the hall, and were so
strongly supported that Faneuil Hall was granted them,
and the meeting was held December 8th, 1837.   Mr.
James T Austin, who was the Attorney-General of
the State, made a violent speech in reply to Dr.
Channing. He declared that Lovejoy was responsible
for his own death, and " died as a fool dieth."   He
compared the Alton mob to the men who threw the

tea into Boston harbor, the slaves to lions, tigers and monkeys, who had to be chained in a menagerie. Then Wendell Phillips arose ; he had not expected to speak, so he tells me. He came in like other spectators ; he went upon the platform and addressed the audience. In the midst of much confusion, he replied with just severity to Mr. Austin, and said among other things, "When I heard him place the murderers of Lovejoy by the side of Hancock, Adams, Otis and Quincy, I thought those pictured lips would have broken into voice to rebuke this recreant American." This was the beginning of the career of Phillips as an anti-slavery orator.

I have in my possession a pamphlet written at that time by Mr. Austin, and will quote a single sentence to show its temper and tone. "'What is to be done in regard to slavery?' I answer, 'Nothing.' It is not desirable that domestic slavery should cease in the United States." I have already shown that the two great political parties were both opposed to the anti-slavery movement ; a large part of the church and the leading theologians were also opposed to it. I will give but one or two examples of this.

Doctor Nehemiah Adams, of Boston, an eminent divine, a man of intelligence and influence, much esteemed by his friends for his personal and good qualities, went to Port Royal, in South Carolina on a visit. On his return he was so unfortunate as to

write a book called " A South-side View of Slavery."
He gave a rose-colored view of that institution ; said
the slaves were contented and happy ; said they had
many privileges, and were treated very kindly ; that
they were not cruelly used ; that he heard them singing in the churches, and he therefore came to the conclusion that the Abolitionists were very much mistaken, and that slavery was not very bad after all.
The evil which seemed to him the most intolerable
was that a Southern gentleman might come to a
Northern State and bring a colored coachman, and
this coachman might be enticed away, and so the
slaveholder would be subject to a good deal of annoy-
ance.   The place where he wrote this book was the
Old Fort Plantation at Port Royal.   There is a large
grove of live oaks there, and in one of them is a seat ;
there he wrote this defence of slavery.   It is a curious
fact that where Dr. Adams composed this book, there
on the 1st of January, 1863, the officer in command
of the United States troops read to a large assembly
of people, white and colored, the Proclamation of
Emancipation by Abraham Lincoln.   A programme
of proceedings had been arranged, but it was interrupted very suddenly.   No sooner had this proclamation been read, than the colored people struck up with
their whole heart, " My country 'tis of thee, sweet
Land of Liberty."   Where they had learned this
hymn I do not know, but they had learned it, and

used it on the first occasion in their lives, when they were able to say in truth, " My Country," and to call it in reality a " Land of Liberty." In this place also Miss Botume, a Northern lady, has during nearly twenty years, taught a large school of colored children. She went down to South Carolina, as many other Northern teachers did. as soon as the capture of the Sea Islands by the battle of Hitton Head, made it possible to teach the colored people. Miss Botume, Miss Towne and other teachers have seen a whole generation of free colored children grow up to a useful manhood under their instructions.

Another Northern man, also a strenuous champion of slavery, was Dr. Lord, President of Dartmouth College. I have two pamphlets of his, the first called, " A Letter of Inquiry to Ministers of the Gospel of all Denominations," and the other " A Second Letter, by Nathan Lord." This gentleman, a president of a New England college, took the ground that slavery is an institution of God according to natural religion ; that it is not opposed to the law of Love or the Golden Rule ; that anti-slavery is a heresy, and a false doctrine ; that slavery is a very useful and wholesome institution ; that it ought to be allowed to extend itself over free territory ; that instead of opposing slavery, Christians should oppose anti-slavery ; and that believing slavery to be a divine ordinance, he

would himself gladly own or hire slaves, if conve-
nient.*

According to Dr. Lord, the great evil was not
slavery but freedom. It was not Pharaoh, but Moses
who was to be blamed ; and, when the prophet Isaiah
said that we must " break every yoke, and let the op-
pressed go free," Dr. Lord would have called his sentiment "a descriptive fallacy," and would have said
that the prophet showed himself "a romantic and excitable person."

Not long after these pamphlets by Dr. Lord, another Christian minister in the Free States came to
the defence of slavery ; and this time it was a bishop
of the Episcopal Church. Bishop Hopkins of Vermont, in 1857 wrote a book called " The American
Citizen." It was a curious farrago, containing a little
of everything. He gave a translation of a part of
Cicero ; he told his readers how to choose a wife, and
opposed the use of salaratus in bread. The bishop,
giving his views on female education, was of the opinion that while it was proper for a young lady to paint
in water-colors, she must by no means be allowed to
paint in oils. He then proceeded to treat of slavery,
maintaining that the slaves were the happiest class of

---

* Compare these declarations with those of Henry Clay, who,
though a slaveholder. declared slavery an evil and a wrong, and said
that nothing on earth would induce him to consent to its going to any
place where it did not exist.

laborers in the world. Like Dr. Lord, he defended
the slave-trade ; and, finally, having proved to his
own satisfaction that slavery was right in itself, sanctioned by Christianity, and even commanded by God,
and was every way a blessed institution, he very
curiously turned round and began to ask how it could
be abolished ! He proceeded to show that it might
easily be brought to an end by sending the whole
colored race back to Africa. If the people of the
United States would pay sixty millions annually for
twenty-five years, we could thus send away 40,000 a
year. He did not say what these emigrants were to
do when they reached Africa, or how they could support themselves there. This was regarded as wisdom
and conservatism in those days. And this was only
six years before the Proclamation of Emancipation.
Was it any wonder when such books as these were
published by the most eminent men in the Northern
churches, that the abolitionists should say in their
haste that the American church was " The Bulwark
of Slavery," "The Refuge of Oppression," and " A
Brotherhood of Thieves ? " And yet the large majority of men in the Northern church were opposed
to slavery, and furnished the recruits for abolition.
But Whittier described well these blind leaders of
the blind, as those who

> "—— tortured the pages of the blessed bible,
> To sanction crime and robbery and blood,

And, in oppression's hateful service, libel
Both man and God.''

Those people in the North who opposed the anti-
slavery movement might thus be classed : First, there
were the political opponents who feared that this
movement would injure the party machine.  The word
" Dough-faces " was invented to describe those among
them who were ready to sacrifice everything to the
South to help their party.  Mr. Calhoun was not a
Dough-face ; he maintained that slavery was right
and necessary.  Southern politicians were manly and
outspoken, and did not conceal their sentiments.  But
some Northern politicians were supple and cunning.
They were aiming at a national office, seeking perhaps the presidency, and they saw very plainly that
the South was so sensitive on the subject of slavery,
and so united, that no Northern man would obtain a
national office unless he went all lengths in showing
his willingness to support the claims of the slave-power.
Their object was to satisfy the South and deceive the
North.  They exhausted all devices to give a plausible
appearance to their concessions to the slave-power.

The most eminent of these leaders were Mr. Buchanan and Mr. Cass.  Perhaps Buchanan went
further than Cass, for the Democrats in Mr. Cass's
state of Michigan were less tractable than those of
Pennsylvania.  At the time Mr. Buchanan was nominated for the presidency I cut from a Richmond paper

an article which said that Mr. Buchanan, from the very first, never failed to vote for every measure the South had demanded, and gave a list of these votes.*

He was rewarded for his complete subserviency to the slave-power by being chosen President in 1856. Whether he found himself happy in the Presidential chair or not, I do not undertake to say. None of his Pro-Slavery votes disturbed the confidence of the Pennsylvania Democrats. The voters of Pennsylvania, of

---

* This is what the Richmond Inquirer said of Mr. Buchanan when a candidate for the Presidency in 1856:

1. In 1836, Mr. Buchanan supported a bill to prohibit the circulation of Abolition Papers through the mail.

2. In the same year he proposed and voted for the admission of Arkansas.

3. In 1836-7 he denounced and voted to reject petitions for the Abolition of Slavery in the District of Columbia.

4. In 1837 he voted for Mr. Calhoun's famous resolutions, defining the rights of the States and the limits of Federal authority, and affirming it to be the duty of the Government to protect and uphold the institutions of the South.

5. In 1838, 1839 and 1840, he invariably voted with Southern Senators against the consideration of anti-slavery petitions.

6. In 1844-5, he advocated and voted for the Annexation of Texas.

7. In 1847, he sustained the Clayton Compromise.

8. In 1850, he proposed and urged the extension of the Missouri Compromise to the Pacific Ocean.

9. But he promptly acquiesced in the Compromise of 1850, and employed all its influence in favor of the faithful execution of the Fugitive Slave law.

10. In 1854 he remonstrated against an enactment of the Pennsylvania Legislature for obstructing the arrest and return of fugitive slaves.

11. In 1854 he negotiated for the acquisition of Cuba.

12. In 1856 he approves the repeal of the Missouri restriction, and supports the principles of the Kansas-Nebraska Act.

13. He never gave a vote against the interest of slavery and never uttered a word which could pain the most sensitive Southern heart.

both parties, have always gladly submitted to the government of the politicians. There was a story among the anti-slavery speakers, about one of their number who once went as a missionary into Bucks county, Va., where there were many German Democrats. He tried to convince his audience that Democracy ought to ally itself to anti-slavery. " Why, what do you call a Democrat ? " said the orator. " Is he not one who believes in equal rights for all ? Is he not one who believes in the freedom of all mankind?" Then an old German cried out, "That's not what I calls a Democrat ; I calls a Democrat a man what votes a Democratic ticket."

There were others who refused to join the anti-slavery ranks, because they feared that this movement would imperil the Union. To this class belonged Mr. Webster, Mr. Everett, and Mr. Choate. Then there were the ecclesiastical opponents, who dreaded lest it should divide the churches. Then came the commercial opponents, who were afraid that it would injure trade. To these were added another class who said, " We have made a contract with the South, and we ought to keep that contract." The result of it was that the political opposition to slavery grew weaker down to the time of the formation of the Republican party. In the early days both the North and South agreed that slavery must be abolished, and that sooner or later it would disappear. The Dane proviso, to exclude it from the Northern territory, was supported, as we have seen, by the Southerners as well as by the Northerners in Congress. But when cotton-growing began to grow profitable, the belief in the abolition of slavery died out at the South. The next view was that it was to divide with freedom the national territory. This opinion asserted itself and triumphed when the Missouri compromise was passed. Then came the determination to extend the domain of slavery by the annexation of Texas. Next it was asserted that slavery was to be prohibited nowhere, but to be maintained everywhere ; that whereever slaveholders went with their slaves, they were to be protected ; and finally that slavery was to command, and liberty to obey. This doctrine was enforced in Kansas so far as they were able by President Pierce and President Buchanan, who made themselves the obedient instruments of the slave-power.

Meantime the anti-slavery movement, an everadvancing stream, "an exulting and abounding river" of thought and action grew deeper, and spread more widely. Among members of Congress it had such advocates as those of whom I have already spoken, Sumner, Chase, John P. Hale, Amos Tuck, Robert Rantoul, Jr., Henry Wilson, John G. Palfrey, Joshua Giddings, Charles Allen of Worcester, Stephen C. Phillips of Salem, Slade of Vermont, Julian of Indiana. Among these, Robert Rantoul of Newburyport, Mass., was one of the greatest promise ; but he was too early lost to his State, and to the nation. A Democrat from conviction and party affiliation, he yet, like John P. Hale of New Hampshire and Morris of Ohio refused to be led by his party to the support or defence of slavery. His speeches show a remarkable power of keen perception, prompt retort, and ready extemporaneous argument. In the latter respect I have scarcely seen his equal. His face was of a Southern type, and his keen eye showed the fire within.

To what has already been said of John Quincy Adams, I will add the following anecdote, received from Capt. Boutelle, of the Coast Survey. He tells me that when he was a very young man, he went to Washington to ask for a position on the Coast Survey. He had one or two letters to John Quincy Adams, and the old gentleman took quite an interest in this youth. " I had heard him called cold," says he, " but if he had been my father he could not have done more for me. He went to the Secretary of the Navy, and waited in the ante-chamber an hour, till he had the opportunity of seeing the Secretary and securing for me the position. The same week, or about that time, the famous ' Latimer petition ' was brought into Congress. Latimer was a fugitive slave who had been arrested and ransomed. This petition was in favor of the right of petition in regard to slavery. It was signed by 300,000 persons, and made an enormous roll. It was placed upon Mr. Adams' desk. in front of him : and as he was rather a short person, only his head appeared above the roll. He said, ' I suppose, Mr. Speaker, it is hardly necessary to send this petition to the desk. It would take two strong men to carry it ; the pages cannot take it. It is a petition headed by George Latimer.' Then a Virginian sprang up and said, ' Does Mr. Adams know who this George Latimer is, who heads that petition ? ' Mr. Adams, who had probably been expecting some such interruption, cried out, in his shrill voice, which rang through the hall, ' Yes I know very well who he is. I have been credibly informed, and I certainly believe the fact, that he is a descendant of one of the first families of Virginia." Latimer was said to be the son of his owner.

Northern men who joined the anti-slavery societies were educated by reading the Liberator, the New York Tribune, the New York Independent, and National Era, all of which papers stood up manfully for the rights of the North, and the cause of freedom. These were sturdy men, and their character cannot be better illustrated than by an anecdote I once heard from Wendell Phillips in regard to a lecture which he was to deliver in some town in New Hampshire. When he arrived at the town, and went to the hall, he was met outside by the President, who said to him, " Mr. Phillips, what are you going to lecture about this evening?" Phillips replied, "Street Life in Europe." "You are not going to lecture on Abolition, then?" He answered, "No sir; I was not asked to do so." "There seems to be some mistake, Mr. Phillips," resumed the President. "No mistake on my part," responded the lecturer; "I was asked to come and give a lecture here to-night, and I have come." "Please to walk into the hall," said the President of the Lyceum. He went on the platform and asked, "Is the Secretary of the Lyceum in the house?" Some one called out "Yes" from the middle of the hall. "I told you, Mr. Secretary, when you wrote to Mr. Phillips, to ask him to lecture to-night on abolition. Did you do so, or did you not?" "I did *not*," was the reply. "Why did you not do it, when the Committee told you to do so?" "Because," returned the other, "I do not mean to have abolition rammed down my throat." To which the President promptly responded, "I will give you to understand, Mr. Secretary, that we do not mean to have you rammed down *our* throats." A vote was taken, and it was decided by a considerable majority that Mr. Phillips should lecture on abolition, and he spoke on that familiar topic during two hours.

Among the citizens of Boston who took part in this anti-slavery movement were many who inherited historic names, like Samuel E. Sewall, who was with Garrison at the beginning, and was faithful to the end.

He is one of the few who remain from that early day of small things. Oliver Johnson was also one of the earliest, and still remains vigorous and active in New York. Mr. Robert Wallcutt was also one of the earliest and most faithful, and is still living. Samuel May, of Leicester, was one who never wavered in his loyalty to the movement. Theodore D. Weld, who by his eloquence is said to have converted most of the theological students in Lane Seminary, Cincinnati, to anti-slavery, and also to have made a convert of James G. Birney, then a slaveholder. and to have induced him to emancipate his slaves, is also still vigorous and active. So is Henry Ward Beecher, whose services in the cause were so very great.

The sons of Dr. Bowditch, the great mathematician; William I. Bowditch and Henry I. Bowditch, both active champions of the slave, are living still. So are Parker Pillsbury, and the two Hoars, with Charles L. Remond and Mr. Buffum   But Edmund Quincy and Horace Mann are gone; and David Lee Child and Lydia Maria Child, Ellis Gray Loring and Louisa Loring, Dr. Follen and Eliza Follen, Wm. Goodell, Francis Jackson, Richard Hildreth, Samuel G. Howe and William Jay. One man whose eloquence then thrilled us is also living, I mean Frederick Douglass, a wonderful proof of the power which is born out of terrible experience. Beside this, Douglass has a great gift of language, and a fine sense of art, which places him among the first orators of our time.  There were great numbers of noble men and women whose names were scarcely heard of, but who were as devoted as those I have mentioned.  They had no care for fame or notoriety, and it was only by accident if they became distinguished.  Such were the two Misses Grimké, who left South Carolina because they could no longer endure the atmosphere of slavery.  Brought up in the Episcopal Church, they left it when they found it wedded to slavery, and joined the Friends and became able advocates of human rights.  Such was Mattie Griffiths and her sister, who left Kentucky for the same reason, emancipating their slaves and leaving themselves without a support.

Many of these admirable men and women have been immortalized in the poems of Whittier, which are like a gallery of portraits—a portrait-gallery devoted to the heroes, saints and martyrs of our time.  There you find the picture of Garrison,—

> " Champion of those who groan beneath
> Oppression's iron hand."

By his side is that of Governor Ritner, of Pennsylvania, the only Northern Governor who, when the slave-power demanded that the Northern States should put down abolition, answered that he " would never submit to give up the free discussion of any subject."

"Thank God for the token—one lip is still free,
 One spirit untrammelled, unbending one knee;
 Thank God that one arm from the shackle has broken;
 Thank God that one man as a freeman has spoken."

And near by is the portrait of Captain Jonathan
Walker, of Massachusetts, who was fined, imprisoned
and branded on the hand for helping slaves to escape
from Florida.

" Welcome home again, brave seaman, with thy thoughtful brow and
                                             [gray,
 And the old heroic spirit of an earlier, better day;
 With that front of calm endurance, on whose steady nerve in vain,
 Pressed the iron of the prison, smote the fiery shafts of pain."

And there is the portrait of Charles Follen, so
sweet and so brave, banished from Europe for loving
freedom *there,* yet keeping his love of freedom *here.*
Not like many others, fleeing from tyranny abroad to
become the allies of tyrants in their new home ; not
like too many of the European patriots, who merely
hated despotism when they themselves suffered from
it. Such a mean-souled patriot was John Mitchell,
who declared that he would like a plantation in
Alabama "stocked with fat negroes." But Follen
was not such a man. He allied himself to the anti-
slavery cause when it was most unpopular, and sacri-
ficed his position in that cause.

"Friend of my soul ! as with moist eye
 I look up from this page of thine—
 Is it a dream that thou art nigh ?
 Thy mild face gazing into mine ?

> " The calm brow through the parted hair,
>   The gentle lips which knew no guile,
>   Softening the blue eyes' thoughtful care
>   With the bland beauty of their smile ? "

And there, in Whittier's gallery, is the portrait of Leggett, the New York journalist, the Democrat who believed in *real* democracy and contended for entire freedom of thought and speech. And there also, in this impartial collection, is Silas Wright, one of the great leaders of the Democratic party, who saw the perils from the slave-power and was man enough to resist it.

> " Man of the millions ! thou art lost too soon."

And then comes Channing, a nobler form—hero and saint in one.

> " In vain shall Rome her portals bar,
>   And shut from him her saintly prize,
>   Whom in the world's great calendar
>   All men shall canonize."

Then comes the picture of the chivalric Torrey, born near Plymouth Rock, and full of the Pilgrim soul. Going to a convention at Annapolis, as a reporter for a Washington paper, and being known as an abolitionist, he was thrust into a prison-cell, and afterward, when delivered, he went to Virginia to aid a family to escape, and was arrested and sentenced to six months in the penitentiary, where he died of hardship and privation. His body was brought to

Boston, and Park Street Church, where his brother worshipped, was refused for the funeral service. He rests in Mount Auburn, and his soul is enshrined by Whittier.

Another picture is of Daniel Neall, a friend of the slave.

> ——" Formed on the good old plan,
> A true, and brave, and downright honest man;
> Who tranquilly in life's great task-field wrought."

And there is the portrait of Robert Rantoul.

> " He who had sat at Sidney's feet,
> And walked with Pym and Vane apart,
> And through the centuries felt the beat
> Of Freedom's march in Cromwell's heart.

> " No wild enthusiast of the right,
> Self-poised and clear, he showed alway
> The coolness of this Northern night,
> The ripe repose of autumn's day."

And there is the best portrait ever taken of Dr. Howe—the hero, the knight, the Bayard of our time —he who fought by the side of Byron in Greece; he who fought with the Poles against Russia; he who stood by the side of the patriots behind the barricades of Paris in 1830; he who helped old John Brown, of Osawatomie, in 1859, and who was the friend of the blind, the deaf and dumb, the sufferers and the weak.

> " Wouldst know him now? Behold him
> The Cadmus of the blind—
> Giving the dumb lips language,
> The idiot clay a mind.

> " Walking his round of duty
>    Sorenely, day by day ;
>    With the strong man's hand of labor
>    And childhood's heart of play.

> " Wherever outraged Nature
>    Asks word or action brave ;
>    Wherever struggles labor
>    Wherever groans a slave.

> " Wherever rise the peoples,
>    Wherever sinks a throne,
>    The throbbing heart of Freedom finds
>    An answer in his own."

And here is the picture of Charles Sumner—in which he is described as combining the scathing power of Brougham, with Canning's grace—described as having been nourished by all the Muses, springing from their arms an athlete to smite the Python of our time ; described as placing on the shrine of freedom the gifts of Cumæ and of Delphi ; and as standing strong as truth, tranquil-fronted, and above all the tumult of earth.

Next, Whittier gives us the sight of Barbour, killed in Kansas by the border ruffians—dying in defence of freedom.

> " Bear him, comrades, to his grave,
>    Never over one more brave,
>    Shall the prairie grasses wave.

> " Bear him up the frozen hill,
>    O'er the land he came to till,
>    And his poor hut roofed with sod.

        Patience friends! the human heart
        Everywhere shall take our part;
            Everywhere for us shall pray

    " On our side are Nature's laws,
    And God's life is in the cause
        That we suffer for to-day.

    " Frozen earth to frozen breast,
    Lay our slain one down to rest,
        Lay him down in hope and faith."

Then we see the fair face and clear eye of Starr
King.

    " The great work laid upon his twoscore years,
    Is done and well done ; if we drop our tears,
    Who loved him as few men were ever loved,
    We mourn no blighted hope, or broken plan
    With him whose life stands rounded and approved
    In the full growth and stature of a man.
    O East and West ! O morn and sunset ! twain
    No more forever !  Has he lived in vain,
    Who, Priest of Freedom, made you one, and told
    Your bridal service from his lips of gold."

When we ask what was the power, what the motive, which united these anti-slavery men, and enabled
them to resist and finally conquer the immense array
of force opposed to them, we must say first that it
was because they had on their side justice and truth,
"and who knows not," said Milton, "that truth is
strong—next the Almighty."

But to this motive was joined another.  Man's
courage and energy is often roused by the very difficulty and danger of the task before him.  Why do
men climb the Matterhorn ; go out to India to shoot

tigers ; go to the North Pole to be frozen in those
awful deserts of cold ; find their way to the sources
of the Nile, or of the Congo ?   Partly, I think, because of the very danger and difficulty of these enter-
prises.   God has put in the human brain the organ
of combat ; not that man shall fight bitter battles
with his brother-man, but that he may fight against
evils, falsehoods, wrongs and cruelties.   Every reformer must have a large organ of combativeness,
and an equally large organ of destructiveness.   Then,
besides all other motives, he is inspired by the joy of
the combat—the dread delight of battle.   A desire to
battle with wrongs and destroy them is not inconsistent with good will towards the wrong-doer.   Such
was the temper of the abolitionists—their words were
sharp, and pointed, and like the Sword of the Spirit
pierced through to the dividing asunder of all sophis-
tries and falsehoods.   But their hearts were kind and
their feelings tender, and those who knew them best
will testify that they were, after all, a good-natured
and affectionate people.

## CHAPTER V.

### ANTI-SLAVERY IN POLITICS.

" Count me o'er earths chosen heroes. They were men who stood
    alone,
While the crowd they agonized for hurled the contumelious stone ;
Stood serene, and down the future saw the golden beam incline
To the side of perfect justice, mastered by their face sublime."
LOWELL.

THERE have been three parties in the United
States which had for their main object to resist the
aggressions of the slave-power by political action.
First came the " Liberty Party " formed in 1840 by
a convention at Albany, presided over by Alvin
Smith, an early abolitionist, and a man of great
ability. It nominated James G. Birney for President,
and at the election which made Gen. Harrison, President, it cast only 7000 votes out of 2,000,000. In 1841,
Salmon P. Chase joined its ranks. In 1843 it held a
convention at Buffalo, which Stephen S Foster said,
" was one of the most earnest, patriotic, and intelligent
bodies which ever met on this continent." In 1844,
it cast 60,000 votes, held the balance in New York,
and defeated Henry Clay, and so caused the election
of Polk and the annexation of Texas—which was proba
bly a great mistake.

The next political anti-slavery party was the " Free-

Soil " party—formed in 1848, to oppose the extension
of slavery into new territories. It met at Buffalo,
August 9, and nominated Mr. Van Buren for the
Presidency and threw 270,000 votes, most of which
being taken from the Democratic party, caused Gen.
Cass to lose the State of New York, and gave the
election to Gen. Taylor. The third political party opposed to Slavery was the " Republican " party, which
Mr. Wilson says was formed and christened in Michigan by a fusion of Free-Soilers and Whigs opposed
to the Kansas-Nebraska bill. This bill passed in
May 1854, repealed the Missouri Compromise, and
admitted slavery into all the territories of the United
States.

July 6th, 1854, a convention in Michigan of Free-
Soilers and Whigs formed a new union and called it
the Republican party. This was followed by a general uprising of the people of the North. It nominated Gen. Fremont for the Presidency. He was
defeated in 1856, by James Buchanan. There were
three candidates, Buchanan, (Democrat) Fillmore,
(American) and Fremont (Republican). Fremont
received 1,340,000 votes. In the next election, in
1860, the Republican party elected Lincoln as President by a popular vote of 1,866,000 against 1,575,000
for Douglas, 847,000 for Breckenridge, and 590,000
for the Bell and Everett ticket. In 20 years it rose
from 7,000 votes to nearly 2,000,000. While these

political anti-slavery movements were going on, the old abolitionists under the lead of Garrison, Phillips and others had decided to oppose all voting and all political efforts under the Constitution. They adopted as their motto, " No Union with Slaveholders." Their hope for abolishing slavery was in inducing the North to dissolve the Union. Edmund Quincy said the Union was " a confederacy with crime " that " the experiment of a great nation with popular institutions had signally failed ; " that the Republic was " not a model, but a warning to the nations ; " that the whole people must be " either slaveholders or slaves ; " that the only escape for " the slave from his bondage was over the ruins of the American Church and the American State ; " and that it was the unalterable purpose of the Garrisonians to labor for the dissolution of the Union." Wendell Phillips said on one occasion, " Thank God, I am not a citizen of the United States." As late as 1861, he declared the Union a failure, and argued for the Dissolution of the Union as " the best possible method of abolishing slavery."*

*Speech in Music Hall, Boston, Jan. 20th, 1861.

"I have recently received a note from Wendell Phillips, in which he says—"I have heard that you said in your lectures something of this kind, that the Garrisonians abstained from voting as one means of abolishing, or *their* means of abolishing slavery—which does not correctly represent us. As I am very proud of the stand we took, and the reason we gave for it, allow me to explain. We abstained from voting because we thought it wrong to do an act which implied

In thus contending for the abolition of slavery by
disunion, and arguing that this was the true anti-
slavery course, we now see that Garrison, Phillips and
their friends were mistaken. Slavery was abolished
not by disunion, but by the power which opposed
disunion. If the North had agreed to disunion and
had followed the advice of Phillips in January 1861,
to " build a bridge of gold to take the Slave States
out of the Union," slavery would probably be still existing in all the Southern States. At all events, it
was not abolished by those who wished for disunion,
but by those who were determined at all hazards and
by every sacrifice to maintain the Union.

Meantime, though the Garrison party were mistaken as to their methods, they contributed a mighty
influence in other ways toward the abolition of slavery. As agitators they were unwearied in pointing
out the evils of slavery. Garrison, Phillips, Quincy,
Wright, Foster, Burleigh, Pilsbury, Buffum—Mrs.

an oath to support the United States Constitution—a Constitution
which we held to be a covenant with Death, and an agreement with
Hell—one that pledged its citizens to help return fugitive slaves,
which we never intended to do, but just the contrary."

No doubt that Mr. Phillips only did what was right and honorable
in refusing to vote while holding these views. He, however, did more.
He advocated the dissolution of the Union. He said (Jan. 15, 1875),
—" For my part I am for the dissolution of the Union, and I seek it
as an abolitionist. I seek it, first and primarily, to protect the slave.
Primarily, it is an Anti-Slavery measure." See also the passage quoted
above from his speech of Jan. 20, 1861. The fact remains that slavery was abolished, not by the Dissolution of the Union, but by those
who resisted its dissolution.

Child, Mrs. Chapman, Lucretia Mott, Abby Kelley, Lucy Stone, Mrs. Follen, Mrs. Ellis Gray Loring, the Mays, the Grimké sisters, and many more, labored incessantly for the object. Though the churches in a large degree were lukewarm, or opposed to anti-slavery—many clergymen of all denominations were actively on the side of this movement. Conspicuous among these were such men as Beriah Green and Henry Ward Beecher ; and among the Unitarian ministers, whom I remember the best as being one of their body, who took an open part in the anti-slavery struggle, I may mention Dr. Channing, John Pierpont, Wm Henry Furness, Theodore Parker, Dr. Follen, Noah Worcester, Dr. Willard, Henry Ware, Jr. John G. Palfrey, Thos. T Stone, Rufus P. Stebbins, Wm. Henry Channing, John T. Sargent, John Parkman, Jr., Caleb Stetson, O. B. Frothingham, Dr. Charles Lowell, Dr. Francis, Geo. F. Simmons, John Weiss, Geo. W. Briggs, Thomas W. Higginson, Fred Frothingham, R. F. Wallcutt, S. R. Craft, Chas. T. Brooks, and others. In 1845, one hundred and seventy Unitarian Ministers signed a protest against slavery, prepared by a Committee appointed for that purpose, of which I was one. It was drawn up by myself, and accepted by the Committee with some slight alterations.*

*The following reminiscences of Dr. Channing by Mrs. Child were written after his death, and published in his Memoirs.

" I shall always recollect the first time I ever saw Dr. Channing in

One of the most eminent opponents of slavery
among the body of the clergy, was Dr. John G. Pal-

private.   It was immediately after I published my "Appeal in favor
of that class of Americans called Africans," in 1833.   A publication
taking broad anti-slavery ground was then a rarity.   I sent a copy to
Dr. Channing, and a few days after he came to see me at Cottage
Place, a mile and a half from his residence on Mt. Vernon Street.   It
was a very bright sunny day ; but he carried his cloak on his arm for
fear of changes in temperature, and he seemed fatigued with the long
walk.   He stayed nearly three hours, during which time we held a
most interesting conversation on the general interests of humanity,
and on slavery in particular.   He expressed great joy at the publication of the 'Appeal,' and added, 'The reading of it has aroused my
conscience to the query whether I ought to remain silent on the subject.'   He urged me never to desert the cause through evil report or
good report.

We afterwards had many interviews.   He often sent for me when I
was in Boston, and always urged me to come and tell him of every
new aspect of the anti-slavery cause.   At every interview I could see
that he grew bolder and stronger on the subject, while I felt that I
grew wiser and more just.   At first I thought him timid, and even
slightly time-serving, but I soon discovered that I formed this estimate merely from ignorance of his character.   I learned that it was
justice to all, not popularity for himself, which rendered him so cautious.   He constantly grew upon my respect, until I came to regard
him as the wisest as well as the gentlest apostle of humanity.   I owe
him thanks for helping to preserve me from the one-sidedness into
which zealous reformers are apt to run.   He never sought to under-
value the importance of anti-slavery, but he said many things to prevent my looking upon it as the only question interesting to humanity.
My mind needed this check, and I never think of his many-sided con-
versations without deep gratitude.   His interest in the subject constantly increased, and I never met him without being struck with the
progress he had made in overcoming some difficulty which for a time
troubled his sensitive conscience.   I can distinctly recollect several
such steps.   At one time he was doubtful whether it was right to pe_
tition Congress on the subject, because such petitions exasperated our
Southern brethren, and, as he thought, made them more tenacious of
their system.   He afterward headed a petition himself.   In all such
cases he was held back by the conscientious fear of violating some

frey.  His father dying in New Orleans, left to his
children his property. a part of which was in slaves.
Dr. Palfrey's brother wrote to him that, as he probably
would not wish to receive slaves as his share, they
would make an arrangement by which his part of the
estate should consist of something else, which he
could conscientiously take.  " No ! " said Dr. Palfrey,
" that would be exactly the same as though I had sold
the slaves.  I prefer to take the slaves, and I propose
to emancipate them."   But he found that he could
not do it without an act of the legislature of Louisiana.
He went to Louisiana and succeeded in getting permission to emancipate them, he took the people to
Boston and by the help of some anti-slavery friends
they soon became able to support themselves.   But
Palfrey was not the man to speak of such things ; he
never said anything about it, but let it drop into forgetfulness as soon as possible.   Another clergyman
who was filled with zeal on this subject was Theodore
Parker, who not only preached continually in regard
to all the events that occurred, but published many
pamphlets and papers in regard to slavery.   I recollect that they began as early as the time of the Mexi-
can war.   There was to be a meeting at that time in
Faneuil Hall to oppose the war, as unnecessary and

other duty while endeavoring to fulfil his duty to the slave.  Some
zealous reformers misunderstood this, and construed into a love of
popularity what was, in fact, but a fine sense of justice, a more universal love of his species."

wrong. The hall was largely filled with men who had
enlisted to go to Mexico, and were there to prevent the
speakers from being heard.    I sat next to Theodore
Parker on the platform. When he attempted to speak
they interrupted him, calling out, " Throw him over !"
He stopped and said, " What good will it do you to
throw me over ? You are men of Massachusetts,
you would not hurt me, I have not the least fear on
that subject ; I shall go home to-night unarmed and
unattended, and none of you here will do me any
harm." Then they cheered him.

I know of churches which were ready from first to
last, always to hear whatever might be said on this
subject on both sides. I have been present in church-
meetings at discussions on slavery at which Mr. Garrison, Mr. Samuel J. May, Horace Greely, and other
anti-slavery men spoke, and were, I remember, replied to by the friends of Mr. Webster, and by those
who strongly opposed abolition.

A rather amusing incident took place in my own
church in Boston, on one occasion. A member of the
society had left us and had gone to Theodore Parker's.
Mr. Parker said to us, " There is a curious man who
has come to my church from yours. He said he
heard so much anti-slavery preaching in your church,
that he meant to leave it and come to mine."

This was rather droll, considering that Theodore
Parker was the most determined and constant anti-

slavery preacher in the city. The motive however, which induced this gentleman to go, was a strong sermon he had recently heard in my pulpit from S. J. May. Shortly after this there was a meeting in Boston of a body of come-outers, who were Non-Residents and Radicals of an extreme type. They could not get a hall in which to hold their meetings and asked leave to occupy our church on Sunday afternoon. It was granted them. I went to see what they were about, and, as I entered, some brother from the rural districts was saying' "all the clergy of the churches are utterly opposed to reform. I do not know what this church is where we are meeting, and I do not know who the minister is, but I venture to say that it is wholly pro-slavery, and that the minister is a pro-slavery man too." I rose and told them the story of this friend who had gone from us to Parker, in order to hear less anti-slavery preaching, and added, "If you have any doubt as to the accuracy of this statement, you can inquire of the man himself for I see the gentleman here this afternoon in this congregation."

In 1850 came the "Compromises," as they were called between the North and the South, between slavery and freedom. They were called Compromises, but as usual their influence was against the cause of liberty. There had been for a long time a bitter struggle on the floor of Congress between the Representatives from the North and the South on the subject of slavery. This ended in a bill proposed by Henry Clay which was supported both by the Whigs and Democrats. After a long struggle which lasted fully four months, these " Compromises," so called, finally passed, and the bill was signed by the Acting President, Millard Fillmore. The object was to put an end to all further discussion in regard to slavery, and to put down all anti-slavery agitation. Both parties pledged themselves to prevent any more discussion. The bill was introduced by Henry Clay on May 8, 1850, and passed Sept. 9, the same year. The particular points were these :

1. That when the time came, four more slave states were to be admitted from Texas.

2. California was to be admitted as a free state.

3. There was to be no Wilmot proviso passed to forbid slavery in the territories.

4. Ten million dollars was to be given to Texas for agreeing to assent to a corrected boundary of New Mexico.

5. The New Fugitive Slave Law was to be made effective, by which slaveholders could more easily recover their fugitive slaves. By that law it was decided that any person claiming a slave might go before any U. S. Commissioner, and by proving to the Commissioner's satisfaction the identity of the man, and that he had escaped from slavery, he could carry him

into slavery without any trial by jury. The question was to be decided by the simple opinion of the U. S. Commissioner on those two points.

6. The last point of the compromise was that the slave *trade* was to be prohibited in the District of Columbia, but slavery was not to be abolished there.

It was at this time that Mr. Webster made his 7th of March speech supporting all these measures. We have not space to discuss here the question of the position of Mr. Webster. It is undeniable that great disappointment was felt at the North, not only by the anti-slavery people, but also by Mr. Webster's personal friends and supporters. It is a fact sufficiently vouched for that Mr. Thomas B. Stevenson, one of Mr. Webster's strongest friends and supporters, was so astonished and confounded when this report came, that he took to his bed for some days. This fact has been publicly stated by Mr. Stevenson's own sister.

The Massachusetts legislature were much agitated by Mr. Webster's speech. Conventions were called to express disapprobation, and the whole feeling in Massachusetts was of great gloom and discouragement. The feeling was that Mr. Webster had gone over from his former position, that he had allied himself to the South, and that his speech was a bid for the Presidency. His course was severely criticised by many leading men of the Whig party, to which he belonged. J. T. Buckingham said in the legislature that he had been a personal friend of Daniel Webster's for thirty years ; that he had looked up to him as a mentor and guide, but " we are now on the opposite sides of the moral universe."

In 1830, when Webster made his great speech in answer to Hayne of South Carolina, I recollect the effect produced on myself as on others, by that famous sentence in which he speaks of Massachusetts.*

I know I felt at that time that to have heard that speech delivered I would willingly have walked from Boston to Washington. And those of my own age who had been brought up with these feelings of reverence for Daniel Webster, and also had been taught by him and others to abhor slavery, naturally felt all the more grieved and wounded, at what seemed to us the apostacy of our great chief. Nothing could better express our feelings than Browning's well known lines on " The Lost Leader," slightly modified thus :

> " We who had loved him so, followed him, honored him,
> Lived in his mild and magnificent eye,
> Learned his great language, caught his clear accents,
> Made him our pattern to live and to die.

* " Mr. President, I will enter into no encomium on Massachusetts. She needs none. There she is. Look at her, and judge for yourselves. There is her history. The world knows it by heart. The past, at least, is secure. There are Concord and Lexington, Boston and Bunker Hill, and there they will stand forever. The bones of her sons, fallen in the great struggle for Independence, lie mingled with the soil of every State, from Maine to Georgia, and there they will lie forever."

"Chatham was for us, Franklin was of us,
  Washington, Jefferson watched from their graves,
He alone, breaks from the van and the freemen—
  He alone sinks to the rear and the slaves."

After the years which have passed, softening all feelings, these words may be too severe. But even now we can read with sympathy Whittier's solemn dirge, repeated by Horace Mann in the House of Representatives, in reference to this 7th of March speech.

"So fallen! so lost! the light withdrawn,
    Which once he wore!
  The glory from his grey hairs gone
    For evermore.

" Revile him not, the tempter hath
    A snare for all!
  And pitying tears, not scorn and wrath,
    Befit his fall.

" O! dumb be passion's stormy rage,
    When he who might
  Have lighted up and led his age
    Falls back in night.

    *    *    *    *    *

" Of all we loved and honored, naugh
    Save power remains,—
  A fallen angel's pride of thought,
    Still strong in chains.

All else is gone; from those great eyes
    The soul has fled;
  When faith is lost, when honor dies
    The man is dead."

Now the friends of Mr. Webster say that this is all unjust; that Mr. Webster was actuated simply by his desire to save the Union and maintain the Constitution, and the rights which the South had under the Constitution ; to keep the contract which the fathers had made, and that it was on this account alone that he made this speech. They say that he felt that the Union stood in great peril, and that he must go as far as he could in doing what might be done in supporting some kind of compromise on which the North and South could unite. There is no doubt that he ought to have the credit of this reasoning. I certainly believe that this was in a large measure the motive which actuated Mr. Webster at the time. Nevertheless there was this conviction in the minds of men that he had made a change, and a great change. He had again and again denounced slavery, and the slave-power. For instance in his first speech on Foote's Resolutions, he said this of Dane's resolution excluding slavery from the Northwest Territories. (Webster's works, vol. 3, page 263.)

"I doubt whether one single law of any lawgiver, ancient or modern, has produced effects of more distinct, marked and lasting a character than the Ordinance of 1787. The instrument was drawn by Nathan Dane, then and now, a citizen of Massachusetts. It fixed forever the character of the population in the vast region northwest of the Ohio, by excluding from them involuntary servitude. It impressed on the soil itself, while yet a wilderness, an incapacity to sustain any other than freemen." Webster calls it "a vast good obtained," "a great and salutary measure of prevention." He asks any intelligent Kentuckian if such an ordinance had been offered to his State when a wilderness, "whether he does not suppose it would have contributed to the ultimate greatness of that commonwealth."

And now it was proposed to affix a similar legal barrier by the Wilmot Proviso to prevent slavery from entering the newly acquired territory of New Mexico and California, and Mr. Webster refuses to do it.

He had said, (Aug. 12, 1848), " I shall consent to no extension of slavery on this continent nor to any increase of slave representation in the other House of Congress." After taking this position, to leave it because he believed that from the conformation of the land in New Mexico, slavery could not enter it, showed a very important change of position. He said that the law of nature, and the law of physical geography settled forever the fact that slavery could not exist in California and New Mexico. But there were silver mining and gold mining in those territories and there has never been a gold or silver mining country where slavery has not been welcome. If the land is fertile, slavery comes in to increase the amount of wealth produced from the soil, as is the case in the cotton regions. If the soil is barren and sterile, slavery comes in to take the hard labor from the hands of the people and put it on the shoulders of the slave. Mr. Webster said, "if a bill were now before us to provide a territorial government for New Mexico, I would not vote to put any prohibition of slavery into it whatever." That was one of the things which shocked the North.

Mr. Webster gave, as his only reason for refusing to exclude slavery by law from the new territories, that it was already excluded by a law of nature, and that he would not uselessly re-affirm an ordinance of nature, or re-enact the will of God. But did not Mr. Webster know that all our laws are meant to carry out the will of God, that when we make a law against theft or murder " we re-enact the will of God ?"

He maintained, however, that this proviso was useless, because the formation of the earth in these territories settled forever that slavery could not exist in California or New Mexico. He explained his meaning by saying, " California and New Mexico are Asiatic in their formation and scenery. They are composed of vast ridges of mountains of great height." If an " Asiatic " conformation could exclude slavery, it is somewhat remarkable that slavery exists now, and has existed for centuries in every country of Asia, as I believe without one exception, unless where it has been abolished by positive enactment of European Governments.

Another serious complaint made against Mr. Web-

ster was this—that after declaring that a trial by jury
ought to be given under the fugitive law, he voted for
Mr. Mason's bill, by which no such right was con-
ferred. In 1848 (Aug. 12), he had said, " It was a
maxim of the Civil Law that between slavery and
freedom, freedom should always be preserved, and
slavery must be proved." " Such, I suppose, is the
general law of mankind." But, by Mr. Mason's bill,
slavery was preserved. and liberty had to be proved.
A colored man, living in a free State, paying taxes as
a free man, regarded by all as free, could be seized
and carried away as a slave without seeing either a
judge or a jury. And this, though the Constitution
of the United States declares that " No one shall be
deprived of life, liberty or property without due process of law."

Mr. Wilson, in his history of the " Rise and Fall of
the Slave-Power," charges Mr. Webster also with
gratuitously volunteering his opinion that Congress
was bound to divide Texas hereafter into four slave-
holding States. I think that this charge, (which I
also on one occasion endorsed in public), can hardly
be maintained, in view of the fact that four new States
were allowed in the joint resolution by which Texas
was annexed to the Union, though it did not deter-
mine that they should necessarily be slave States."

Now we might consider that Mr. Webster was actuated by a desire to preserve the Union from danger

and dissolution, and to do justice to the provisions of the Constitution if he had done no more than this. But he did a great deal more. The anti-slavery people always said that one of his motives was a desire to be President of the United States, and his friends have admitted that fact. They have admitted not only that he desired to be President of the United States, but that he was very much disappointed in not getting a nomination. A pamphlet has lately been published containing the address of Mr. Stephen M. Allen, President of the Webster Historical Society, made at the Webster Centennial. October 12, 1882. In this address, Mr. Allen says, " That Daniel Webster wanted to be President of the United States, I concede. But that was a laudable ambition." " He believed to his dying day that if the people had had their own way, unbiased by selfish and jealous party-leaders, he would have been elected President of the United States."

But if Mr. Webster had fixed his heart on that position, what follows ? That he must have known, perfectly well, by his long experience in Washington, that no one could be elected President in 1852 but by the consent of the slave-power. He knew that the slave-power would not consent to the election of any man who did not show to them that he was on their side in their determination to extend slavery into all the territories, and to maintain it by all means where it existed. He could not have hoped for a nomination unless he was willing to show them that he would go as far as any other leading Whig to satisfy them on these points, and that he was able and willing to defend their interests more powerfully than any other man who could be nominated. He made quite a number of campaign speeches, in which he violently denounced the anti-slavery party, abused the abolitionists, called them a " rub-a-dub " party, and said many other similar things. When speaking in Virginia he said that the higher law was an absurdity. " What is the higher law? " said he. " How high is it ? Is it higher than the Blue Ridges ? Higher than the Alleghany Mountains? " It seems impossible to believe that a man of his great intelligence could have said such things as this, unless his motive was to please the South and to obtain the next presidential nomination.

But, after all, we must remember his great services. The power which he exercised in creating and maintaining a Union sentiment was certainly one great factor in the war for Union and Freedom. There were two great forces which united to enable the North to conquer—the love of the Union and the love of Freedom. Mr. Webster had contributed mightily to create that love of the Union which resisted Secession, and which sternly opposed the dissolution of that Union. Meantime, the anti-slavery movement, led by Garrison and his friends, with the aid of the great political anti-slavery parties, had done as much to create an abhorrence of slavery and its extension. And these two great forces united in their opposition to Secession, which struck its blow at once against Union and against Freedom. The dissolution of the Union would have perpetuated slavery. There certainly has never been in this country any other public man who had such a commanding genius as Daniel Webster—never one who had so much reserved force. One of the most pathetic and tragic features of the whole affair was that he never seemed to have a cause equal to his capacity, and that the only cause which would have been sufficiently great to bring out all his ability was the anti-slavery movement. If he had put himself at the head of the movement, all other intellects would have paled before the majesty of his intelligence. Mr. Bryant on one occasion, in the Evening Post, quoted Milton's description of one of the rebel angels, applying it to Mr. Webster, and the description of his person and bearing is very accurate.

> " With grave
> Aspect he rose, and in his rising seemed
> A pillar of state. Deep on his brow engraved
> Deliberation sat and public care,
> And princely counsel in his face yet shone,
> Majestic though in vain. Sage he stood,
> With atlantean shoulders fit to bear
> The weight of mightiest monarchies. His look
> Drew audience and attention still as night
> And summer's noontide air, while thus he spoke."

If this description had been written expressly for
Mr. Webster, it could not have been more exact.
Probably, Milton, who was in London during the de-
bates of the Long Parliament, meant to give recollec-
tions of Pym's oratory in these lines, and that of
Wentworth in the description of Belial.

There never was so dark a time in the history of
this conflict as after these compromises of 1850. Mr.
Webster's speeches exercised an immense influence
to check the whole anti-slavery movement. It was
agreed by the leaders of public opinion that nothing
more should be said on the subject ; the anti-slavery
men must be silenced. And then a woman spoke,
and the whole world began again to talk about slavery.
Uncle Tom's Cabin was printed in the National Era
in numbers between the 5th of June 1851 and April
1st, 1852, while Mr. Gamaliel Bailey was editor. He
had written to Mrs. Stowe, asking if she could not
write a story bringing in facts about slavery, long
enough to fill a column or two, in two or three successive numbers of the Era. But it grew under her
hands until it resulted in the most popular work of
modern times. It was published in book form in
1852. In eight weeks 100,000 copies were sold ; in
a year 200,000. In 1856, 313,000 had been circu-
lated. In London thirty editions were published in
six months. In the British Museum, there are forty-
three different editions in English. In 1852 one

million copies had been sold in England. All over
Europe the book had a like rapid and large success.
Translations were made into French, German, Dutch,
Italian, Russian, Magyar, Wallachian, Welsh, Danish,
Swedish, Portuguese, Spanish, Polish, Armenian,
Arabic, Chinese, and Japanese. There are more
than fifty-five different translations of this book now
in the British Museum. It was one of the most wonderful successes in literature. I was travelling in
Europe a year or two after it was written, and was
told in some bookstores in Germany and Italy, that
they found it difficult to publish any other novels.
They sold nothing but " Uncle Tom," or some other
book connected with it. In every picture-gallery, we
saw scenes from " Uncle Tom's Cabin." It was said
that a colored man obtained a great deal of success in
England by pretending that he was " George," and
that he had just got back from Liberia. This novel
seemed almost like a work of inspiration. It was
full of accurate knowledge of the South, although
Mrs. Stowe had scarcely been in any of the Slave
States. Her pictures of southern life were vivid and
charming. The story was intensely interesting ;
justice was done to the kind masters and slaveholders.
Slave manners and customs were graphically painted ;
plantation scenes vividly described. The terrible
tragedy of the book was relieved by fortunate escapes,
by droll incidents and frequent touches of quiet

humor. What can be better, for instance, to mention one out of many points, than the account of the Ohio Senator who is introduced arguing with his wife that slaves must be returned to their owners, that it is highly improper not to execute the fugitive slave law ; and then when the door opens and the poor runaway slave-girl comes in, what does this senator do but tackle up his horse and wagon and carry her to the nearest station on the underground Railroad? It is a book to rank forever with the five or six immortal stories which will never die, Don Quixote, the Pilgrim's Progress, Robinson Crusoe, Gulliver's Travels, the Vicar of Wakefield. Its influence in the progress of the movement was great but quite incalculable. A flood of light was thrown upon the question of slavery. It was held up before all mankind, and the power of the public opinion of the world was brought to bear on it. Everything else that was ever written on this subject sinks to comparative insignificance beside this book. It reaches the common heart of ·man, in cot or castle, in Arctic zone or African sands.

A pamphlet by Austin Bearse, "Reminiscenses of Fugitive Slave Law days in Boston, 1880,"—contains an account of the Vigilance Committee in that city, which was organized to protect fugitives from slavery and keep them from being returned. The names of the officers and members are given, including many

of the best men of the city,  The pamphlet describes
in a vivid manner the sufferings and heroism of the
fugitives, and the way in which they were taken care
of by this Committee.   He mentions that when Mrs.
Stowe was about to write her "Key to Uncle Tom's
Cabin," she was taken by Mr. R. F Walcutt and Mr.
Bearse to Lewis Hayden's house, where she saw
thirteen newly escaped slaves.

Another interesting pamphlet, published in 1864
by James McKaye, Esq., as a report to Mr Stanton,
is called " The emancipated  slave, face to face with
his old master."   Mr. McKaye was one of the commission appointed by Secretary Stanton to obtain information concerning the past and present condition
of the colored people in the slave states   Its account
of the cruelties inflicted on slaves is too harrowing
to be more than referred to.   One story. however,
will bear repeating.   It is of Octave Johnson, who
was in 1864 a corporal in the *Corps d'Afrique.*   His
owner, a Mr. Coutsell of Louisiana, had ordered him
to be whipped severely for falling asleep over his
work.   Octave had never been whipped, and immediately ran for the swamp.   He was a very fast run-
ner, and escaped his pursuers, and after some days
found a band of refugees in the depths of the jungles.
His master, determined not to lose him, hired a
famous professional slave-hunter with a pack of
twenty hounds to recover him.   Notice of this was

given in advance to the fugitives who put their
women in a place of safety, rubbing the soles of their
feet with the blood of rabbits to deceive the hounds,
and then waited their coming with clubs. They
killed eight of the dogs, slowly retreating as they
fought. Toward sundown, being completely exhausted and torn by the teeth of the dogs, they scattered
and fled. Octave and some of his companions ran
for a bayou, which they found full of alligators. They
scrambled across, over roots and fallen trees and escaped. The hounds followed, but the alligators, not
attacking the negroes, killed six of the dogs, and the
rest were recalled. Octave being asked why it was
that the alligators had spared the men, replied,
"Dunno, Massa. Some of 'em said dey tought it
was God made 'em do it ; but 'pears to me de alligators loved dog's flesh better'n *personal flesh.*"

Octave lived in the swamp with this party of ten
women and twenty men for eighteen months. At the
end of that time New Orleans fell into the hands of
the Union troops, and it became the turn of the masters to escape.

But perhaps the most interesting narratives of escaped slaves is to be found in Mrs. Child's " Life of
Isaac Hopper." Mr. Hopper, a member of the Society
of Friends, was the protector during many years, of
the escaped fugitives who came to Philadelphia. By
his courage, coolness, knowledge of law, tact and

readiness of mind, he almost always found some way to baffle the slave-hunter.

To the slaveholder, brought up to regard slaves as his lawful property, all such proceedings seemed wholly unjustifiable. To help a fugitive to escape was to them the same as taking so much money out of their purse. But to most Northern men the right of every man to his own freedom was a self-evident truth. If told that the Constitution and laws forbade helping a fugitive to escape, they appealed to "the higher law," recognized by the greatest jurists as superior to human enactments. They quoted the declaration of the apostles to the Jewish authorities,— "Whether it be right in the sight of God to harken unto you more than unto God, judge ye."

Once when the minds of the community were occupied with these discussions, I was expecting a visit from some relatives, a gentleman and his wife, natives of Georgia, and slaveholders. All my family were strictly warned not to say a word about slaves or slavery. But this Southerner had hardly been in the house half an hour before he introduced the subject, and we spent the whole evening in an earnest, but amicable discussion. Among other things, he asked me how I, as a Christian, could help slaves to escape when the Apostle Paul, in the epistle to Philemon, had set the example of sending one back into slavery. I requested him to read the epistle with me, calling

his attention to the passage in which Paul asked Philemon to receive back this fugitive, " not now as a servant, but above a servant, a brother beloved." I told
my Southern friend that I would readily send back a
fugitive, if I could depend on his not being received
as a slave, but as a brother. The good Georgian,
being a man of candor, admitted that the tone of
this epistle was not much of a support to the fugitive
slave law.

When combustible substances have been accumu.
lating for years, a single flash of lightning will set
them into flames. This flash was the raid of John
Brown at Harper's Ferry. He has been often charged
with going there to excite an insurrection among
the slaves. Such was not his intention. His purpose was to run off gangs of slaves into Pennsylvania
and make them free, in order to make slavery insecure
in the border states. I first saw John Brown at
Charles Sumner's house in Hancock street, Boston.
I called to see how Mr. Sumner was. I was shown
to his chamber, where he was reclining on the bed.
Three men were in the room with him, Captain John
Brown, one of his sons, and James Redpath. In the
course of the conversation the circumstances of the
assault on Sumner were referred to, and he said,
" The coat I had on is hanging in that closet." John
Brown went to the closet, took out the coat, and look-
ed at it as a devotee would contemplate the relic of a

saint.  Mr. Sanborn in his life of of John Brown, says this was the only time in which he and Sumner are known to have met.

Then came the days of John Brown, of Oswatomie. He appeared in Kansas resisting the attacks of the Missourians.  He was brought up in the hatred of slavery.  He was born in Torrington, Conn., in the year 1800, and taken to the Western Reserve in 1805 by his father, who was an anti-slavery man and an Old Testament Christian.  John Brown believed in fighting, as the saints of the Old Testament believed in it, and he went to Kansas taking with him six sons simply for the purpose of aiding the people of Kansas to make that a free state.

In 1858, I met him in Dr. Howe's office.  He was then arranging his raid on Harper's Ferry.  He said that he was proposing to do something which should alarm the slaveholders along the northern line of slavery, and make them feel that they could not hold their slaves in safety, and so induce them to move South, and he hoped thus, by a series of attacks along the border, that slavery would gradually be pushed further South, and all the rest of the territory would be free soil.  That was his plan.  He said, "I am proposing to do on a larger scale what I did in Kansas. When I found that the Missouri people were in the habit of attacking us in Kansas, I saw that we must fight fire with fire.  So I organized a party and in-

vaded Missouri, and carried off a whole party of slaves
some 20 or 30. I took them into Kansas, and marched them through Nebraska and Iowa into Illinois, and
finally carried them over into Canada, where they
were free. Though the papers told every day where
we were, yet on one occasion only was I hindered
on my march. I was crossing into Nebraska, when
the United States marshal came into the hut or log
cabin where I was with only a few men, and ordered
me to give up the slaves to him, and to his orders.
I took my rifle," said old John Brown, "and I told
him I would give him two minutes to leave in, and no
more. But if I had known he was one of the men
who murdered my friends in Kansas, I wouldn't have
given him those two minutes." The next day the
marshal, with a large posse of men waited for Brown's
party to cross the river. John Brown had only about
20 men. He formed his men into two lines; and
they charged into the river, and by the time they had
reached the other side the marshal's party broke and
ran. Brown's men pursued, caught the marshal, made
him dismount, and put an old colored woman and her
baby on his horse, which they compelled him to lead
during the rest of the day.

The following incident was related to me by General
Carrington:

" When I was a boy and went to school in Torrington, there came into the schoolroom one day a tall

man, rather slender, with grayish hair, who said to the boys : ' I want to ask you some questions, in geography. Where is Africa ? ' ' It is on the other side of the ocean, of course,' said a boy. ' Why " of course " ' asked the man. The boy couldn't say, ' why " of course. " ' Then the man proceeded to tell them something about Africa and the negroes, and the evil of the slave trade, the wrongs and sufferings of the slaves, and then said, ' How many of you boys will agree to use your influence, whatever it may be, against this great curse, when you grow up ? ' They held up their hands. He then said that he was afraid some of them might forget it, and added, ' Now I want those who are *quite sure* that they will not forget it, who will promise to use their time and influence toward resisting this great evil, to rise.' Another boy and I stood up. Then, this man put his hands on our heads, and said, ' Now may my Father in heaven, who is your Father, and who is the Father of the African ; and Christ, who is my Master and Saviour, and your Master and Saviour, and the Master and Saviour of the African ; and the Holy Spirit, which gives me strength and comfort when I need it, and will give you strength and comfort when you need it, and which gives strength and comfort to the African,— enable you to keep this resolution which you have now taken.' And that man was John Brown."

I have in my possession two autograph letters

written by him in prison, before his execution ; one
to Mrs. Marcus Spring, who went to Virginia to offer
him whatever comfort or assistance he might need.
In this note he thanks her warmly for her kindness,
and invokes on her the blessing of the God of his
fathers. In the other he writes to a clergyman whom
he knew and esteemed. He tells him that he is at
perfect peace ; that his death will do more than his
life would have done, and he should on the whole be
sorry to be released, because if he lived he might do
something which would let him down to a lower level
than that on which he had previously lived.

We remember how when John Brown was being
led to execution, he remarked on the beauty of the
scenery. He saw on the way a colored woman with
a colored infant in her arms. He took the colored
infant in his arms and kissed it. Only a few months
after that, I was riding through Virginia woods by
moonlight, and a regiment of Wisconsin soldiers were
marching by, singing, " John Brown's body lies moul-
dering in the ground. His soul is marching on." And
his soul was marching on. It marched on until the
whole South was redeemed.

## CHAPTER VI.

### THE COMBAT DEEPEN

"Up to our altars, then,
   Haste we, and summon
Courage and loveliness
   Manhood and voman!
Deep let ur pledges be,
   Freedom forever!
Truce with oppression?
   Never, O, never!"
                        WHITTIER.

THE compromises of 1850 were intended to settle the question between slavery and anti-slavery for all time. But it is a mistake to suppose that you can compromise principles. It is always right and proper to effect compromises if possible between opposing *interests*, but not between opposing *principles*. In the latter case it is saying "Peace! Peace! where there is no peace." It is as the scripture forcibly puts it, "daubing a wall with untempered mortar, so that when a fox runs up on it, he will break it down."

Scarcely had these compromises of 1850 been arranged when the war of tongue and pen, and political

action, recommenced and raged more violently than
over. During the next ten years, from 1850 to 1860,
the slave-power gained many victories. It elected
Pierce in 1852 and Buchanan in 1856. They were
both Northerners and both were subservient to the
slave-power. The slaveholders had found that the
Southern men, like Zachary Taylor, though slaveholders, were not so submissive to their dictation, as
northern men like Pierce and Buchanan.

The slaveholders had secured the repeal of the
Missouri Compromise of 1820, which had divided the
territories between slavery and freedom. This start-
ling event opened Kansas and Nebraska to slavery.
This was accomplished under the lead of Stephen A.
Douglas, an eminent northern Democrat. He took
the ground which was called "Squatter Sovereignty;" namely, that the people of the territory were
themselves to decide whether they would allow slavery
to exist among them when the territory became a
state. Congress was not allowed to prohibit slaveholders from settling with their slaves in any place,
while under territorial government. Of course, it
was intended and expected that when the time came
for adopting a state constitution, slavery would be
already there, and the territory would become a slave
state as a matter of necessity. Under the influence
of Stephen A. Douglas this law of "Squatter Sovereignty" was pressed through Congress, and this was

Mr. Douglas' offer for the presidency. He gave to the slave-power *all the territories*, to be turned into slaves states.

The next act of the slave-power was to establish the Lecompton Constitution in Kansas. This constitution had been formed by Missouri slaveholders who had gone into Kansas and taken possession of the polls. They had, to support them, the whole strength of the executive power under Pierce and Buchanan, and they used it as far as they could to put down freedom in Kansas. The history of the Kansas struggle is still to be written. It is full of lights and shades, heroisms and villany, tragic adventure and romantic exploits. As Kentucky was the "dark and bloody ground" in an earlier day, so Kansas was the dark and bloody ground during the conflict of freedom and slavery. It was a struggle between powers so unequal that it seemed like desperation on the part of the anti-slavery party to hope for success. The slaveholders of Missouri, close at hand and far more numerous than the Kansas population, invaded the territory, massacred the free settlers, took possession of the polls, elected a slaveholders's legis lature and formed a slave state constitution. A Congress controlled by the slave-power, and two presidents, accepted these acts as legal, and gave the military forces of the Union to enforce them. This was the outcome of " Squatter Sovereignty "—that neither the squatters nor the bona fide settlers in Kansas were permitted to form their own Constitution ; Congress had abdicated in favor of the border ruffians of Missouri.

But the free state settlers of Kansas were not easily discouraged. They knew they had right on their side, and were determined to maintain it. Their right was so clear, indeed, that a number of governors, selected and appointed by Presidents Pierce and Buchanan, with the purpose of putting down freedom, were converted by the sight of the terrible facts, and became opposed to the slaveholders' iniquity. Like Balaam they went to curse, and they remained to bless. So it was with Governor Reeder, who was opposed to free soil when sent out as governor in 1854. He ordered an election for the legislature. The Missourians came across the line, took possession of the polls, and chose the legislators. This was more than Governor Reeder could bear, and he set aside the election. For this he was removed by Pierce, and Shannon appointed in his place, who made a speech on his way, to the Missouri people, telling them he was in favor of slavery in Kansas. But he, too, was converted by the sight of the cruel persecutions and murders inflicted on the people of Kansas, and was therefore removed, and Governor Geary appointed. He also became disgusted, and resigned, and Robert J. Walker was then made governer, Walker had been in high favor with the slave-power, but he too resigned, not finding himself willing to do the work required of him by President Buchanan. Meanwhile, in spite of opposition, the free state settlers had poured into Kansas in such numbers that they were becoming as numerous as the invaders from Missouri, and able to hold their own against them, in battle.

For the condition of things in Kansas was that of war. Those who find fault with Captain John Brown of Osawatomie for fighting fire with fire, should re. member the murders and assassinations of the free state men, which were being done with impunity. John Brown was an Old Testament hero, who believed in retaliation, and was determined that these murders should cease. He resisted the invaders, and defeated them in the field. He also approved of killing those who had murdered free state men in cold blood, and who could not be punished by law. In this I think him wrong.

The people of the North determined that slavery should be excluded by the majority of the inhabitants. Emigration aid societies were formed in Massachusetts, which sent colonists to Kansas to make it a free state. In July, 1854, one of these founded Lawrence ; another followed and founded Topeka. As soon as it was understood that this was being done, the people of Missouri invaded Kansas and attempted to drive the free settlers away. They entered Kansas again and again, as we have seen, at the time of elections, and elected a pro-slavery delegate to Congress ; and this was done by the advice of a Senator from Missouri.

The free-state men met at Topeka and formed the Topeka Constitution in October, 1855.

The Missourians continued to enter Kansas and to murder the free-state men. One man named Barber, an unoffensive man, was shot down by an Indian agent named Clark, for refusing to follow him when ordered to do so. Yet, though this was well known, President Pierce retained this man in office. The Missouri people attempted to destroy Lawrence, but Governor Shannon permitted the residents to arm and protect themselves. Thereupon the Missourians denounced Shannon as an abolitionist, and he was removed. In 1856, Col. Buford brought from the South to Kansas a regiment, with the avowed purpose of driving out the free-state men. The President and Senator Douglas supported the invaders. In May, the town of Lawrence was attacked by the Missouri slaveholders, and the hotel, printing offices, and other buildings were destroyed. The free state legislature was dispersed by Col. Sumner, an officer of the United States army, under orders from Washington. He told the members that it was contrary to his own feelings and wishes, but he was obliged to do so under positive orders from the President.

In 1857, the Lecompton Constitution was adopted by a convention chosen by the Missourians. President Pierce maintained that this was the true constitution for Kansas, although he knew that it was formed entirely by those who were from outside the State. He knew that a great majority of the people wanted to make it a free state. This Lecompton Constitution passed Congress under the influence of Pierce and the Democrats ; but the people of Kansas refused to accept it. They were supported by the people of New England. There was a free state league, which met at the house of Dr. Samuel Cabot in Boston. He was the President. It sent out Sharp's rifles to enable the people to defend themselves. George L. Stearns was another friend of John Brown who aided the cause of freedom in Kansas with great generosity. Another free-state league was formed with Mrs. Cabot at the head, which sent out food and clothing from all parts of New England. This was brought to Boston and forwarded to Kansas. These efforts had much to do with the final result, which caused Kansas to become a free State.

On the 19th and 20th of May, 1856, Charles Sumner delivered his speech in the United State Senate on the " Crime against Kansas." It combined argument and invective, and exposed in plain language the cruel injustice done to the free citizens of Kansas by the United States Government. Whittier said "it was the severe and awful truth, which the sharp agony of the national crisis demanded." The slaveholders in Congress were excited to madness by this exposure, and to inflict personal injury on Sumner was the only answer in their power. Sumner was assaulted in his seat, as he was writing, after the adjournment of the Senate, by Preston S. Brooks, of South Carolina. The injuries were so severe that it was four years before he took his seat again in the Senate, during which time Massachusetts left his chair empty.* If this atrocious attack on the freedom of speech in Congress had been the work of a single assassin, as was the murder of Lincoln by Booth, it would have been less injurious to the Southern interests. But while the South repudiated Booth, it endorsed Brooks. Brooks was censured by a majority of the House, resigned his seat, and was triumphantly re-elected. His action in assaulting Sumner was applauded by the Southern press with almost entire unanimity. He was presented with canes; he was congratulated by Southern statesmen. Toombs, Jefferson Davis, Mason, expressed their entire approval of his course. President Buchanan, while he called Sumner's speech "the most vulgar tirade of abuse ever delivered in a repre-

* As Tacitus says of the absent statues of Brutus and Cassius at the funeral of Junia, he was the more conspicuous because not there.

sentative body, added that " Mr. Brooks was incon siderate."

This murderous assault on freedom, in the person of its defender, like every other triumph of the slave-power, was in reality a defeat and a disaster. Many who before had stood aloof from the anti-slavery movement, now made up their minds that resistance to the lawless arrogance of the slaveholders, had become a matter of necessity.

Mr. Sumner once showed me an " Album Amicorum," such as were kept by Europeon scholars at the revival of learning, in which to receive the autographs of their brother scholars throughout Europe. The one in the possession of Charles Sumner contained some lines in the handwriting of John Milton. They consisted of his name—the two last lines of Comus :—

> " Or, if virtue feeble were,
> Heaven itself would stoop to her."

and the Latin line, slightly modified thus—

> "Cœlum, non animam, muto, cum trans mare curro."

Sumner, when he showed me this autograph, told me he was especially desirous of possessing an autograph of Milton, because of what happened after his injury. He was much discouraged one day, and thought he should never be able to resume his seat in the Senate. But taking up a volume of Milton, his eye fell on Milton's sonnet on his blindness, and it encouraged Sumner, as if Milton were himself speaking to him from another world,—

"What supports me, dost thou ask?
The conscience, friend, to have lost them, overplied
In liberty's defence, my noble task
Of which all Europe rings from side to side."

Another victory of the slave-power was won in 1857, when the Supreme Court of the United States decided by the mouth of Chief Juctice Taney, that Congress had no right to forbid the extension of slavery through the territories of the Union, and that no colored person could be a citizen of the United States, if his ancestors had ever been slaves ; consequently no free colored man, though a citizen of Massachusetts under its laws, could sue or be sued in the United States Courts. This paper defied the facts of history by saying that when the Constitution was formed the colored people were regarded as of an inferior order, and " *having no rights which the white men were bound to respect.*" Judge Taney declared that the signers of the Declaration of Independence regarded the blacks *only as property,* not as persons. When he wrote this, Judge Taney had before him the declaration of Jefferson, Franklin, and others of their generations, on the injustice of holding colored men as slaves. The court then decided that the Missouri Compromise, and all other acts of Congress restricting slaveholders from carrying their slaves into the territory of the Union, were unconstitutional.

It was a satisfaction to some of us in Massachusetts, that Judge Benjamin R. Curtis dissented from this

opinion, and demolished the argument of the Chief
Justice by the weight of facts which could not be
denied and a logic which could not be resisted.  We
who were fellow-citizens, fellow-classmates, and aware
of the ability of Judge Curtis, were thankful that he
was then on the bench to destroy the sophisms and
expose the ignorance of Judge Taney.

The Fugitive Slave Law of 1850, passed as a part
of the  Compromise," was liable to very grave objections.  The Constitution of the United States declares
that " in suits at common law, where the value of con-
troversy exceeds twenty dollars the right of trial by
jury shall be preserved," and that "no one shall be
deprived of life, liberty and property without due
process of law."  But by the action of the Fugitive
Slave Law, a colored man in a free state, living as a
free man, might be seized as a slave and taken into
Southern slavery without seeing either a judge or a
jury.  Such cases occurred.  In one case a colored
man, Adam Gibson, was seized as a slave in Pennsylvania, and surrendered by Edward D. Ingraham,
United States Commissioner, with indecent haste.
He was taken to Elkton, Maryland.  There the supposed owner, Mr. William T. Knight, refused to
receive him, saying he was not the man, and he was
restored to freedom.  In this instance the slaveholder
was far more honorable than the United States Commissioner.  But this case showed how easy it was for

a free colored man to be kidnapped under this law.
Mr. Webster had said "there is no danger of any such
violation" (by a false claim) "being perpetrated." In
five months after Mr. Webster had given this re-
assuring promise, the above case of a false claim and
delivery of a free man into slavery took place. In
fact, under this law, the kidnapping of free persons
became a regular business. The courts decided that
a man *claiming* a slave had the right to seize him
without a warrant and take him away. Oliver Anderson, a colored man living near Chillicothe, Ohio, was
dragged from his house in the night of October 11th,
1859, and carried to Kentucky without any examina-
tion or trial. Two Ohio kidnappers who assisted the
Kentuckian, were tried and acquitted on the ground
that under the Prigg decision, a master, (or one claim
ing to be an owner) may seize his slave, and call any
person to help him and take him away, without any
process of law. In all these decisions it was assumed,
*prima facie*, that the person claimed as a slave must
be a slave, and the person claiming him, the owner.
This was the tacit assumption of the Fugitive Slave
Law itself. The possibility that the person seized
might be a free man, falsely claimed, was quietly
ignored. A tract was published by the American
Anti-Slavery Society, called "The Fugitive Slave Law
and its victims," which gives the names of hundreds
of colored people taken from the North into slavery

under this law in the ten years following its enactment.
The place, date and circumstances are given in each
case.

The most important cases in Boston were those of
Shadrach, (February, 1851), Thomas Sims, (April,
1851), and Anthony Burns, (May, 1854). Shadrach
was rescued, Sims was delivered by the decision of
George Ticknor Curtis, Burns by that of Edward G.
Loring.   Probably, few things made so many con-
verts in Boston to anti-slavery as these events.   It
brought the matter home to the people.   It so happened that to prevent a rescue in the case of Sims,
the court house was surrounded by heavy chains,
which seemed the natural symbol of the degradation
of Massachusetts and her laws.

After the rescue of Shadrach, several persons were
indicted for the offence in the United States court.
One of these was Lewis Hayden, himself a fugitive
slave, who had escaped from Kentucky in former
years.   I had the pleasure of becoming acquainted
with him when he first came to Boston.   He told one
evening the story of his slavery and escape, in the
church of which I am the pastor, and moved us all
deeply by the pathos of his narrative.   At the time of
the rescue of Shadrach I was residing in Western
Pennsylvania, and hearing of the indictment of Mr.
Hayden, wrote to him expressing my sympathy.   In
reply, I received the following characteristic letter,

written at his request by John A. Andrew, afterwards
the war governor of Massachusetts.

BOSTON, 5th March, 1857.

DEAR FRIEND :—

Lewis Hayden received a line from you
last evening which he begged me to answer in his behalf, and to express for him the gratitude he feels for
the kindness and sympathy you entertain towards
him. It gratified him, beyond measure, that you
should thus remember him. He is bound over to answer to the next term of the United States district
court. But I have no idea that he, or any other person, will be convicted. The poorest colored man
finds no difficulty in procuring bail at a moment's
warning. I think there is a reaction commencing.
. . . The rescue of Shadrach was a noble thing—
nobly done. . . . The thing was the result of the
extemporaneous effort, energy and enthusiasm of one
old man, a personal friend of Shadrach, who stimu-
lated by his own stubborn zeal the few with whom he
came in contact, to follow him in his determination to
save his friend (whose horror of a return to slavery he
had always known) from the hands of the law, at whatever personal hazard. That man will never be found.
Indeed, all the principal actors are, as I understand,
beyond the reach of process.

God grant that no man may ever be sent from
Massachusetts into the prison house of slavery. I

hate war and love peace ; but I should less regret the death of a hundred men defending successfully the sacred rights of human nature and the blood-bought liberties of freemen, alike cloven down by this infernal law, than I would the return to bondage of a single fugitive.

Your friend,

JOHN A. ANDREW.

The prayer of John Andrew was not granted ; Sims and Burns were both remanded to slavery. But the excitement produced by these renditions created many new and determined foes to this aggressive system. I read, in Western Pennsylvania, the terrible denunciation of " The Sims Commissioner," from the platform in the Music Hall, where Theodore Parker, every Sunday, poured forth his floods of fiery eloquence. At the rendition of Burns I was in Boston. I saw the crowds assembled in State Street and Washington Street on that gloomy day, when the slave-power triumphed, as George the Third triumphed at Bunker Hill. " One more such victory," they might have said, " and we are ruined." I saw, from the window of John A. Andrew's chambers, the lawyers' offices hung with black. I saw the cavalry, artillery, marines and police, a thousand strong, escorting, with shotted guns, one trembling colored man to the vessel which was to carry him to slavery.

I heard the curses, both loud and deep, poured on these soldiers; I saw the red flush in their cheek as the crowd yelled at them, "Kidnappers! Kidnappers!" It was evident that a very trifling incident might have brought on a collision, and flooded the streets with blood.

Meantime, in the ten years which preceded the civil war, the anti-slavery cause won a succession of moral as well as political victories.

The publication of Uncle Tom's Cabin, not only electrified the whole world, but poured a flood of light into the mysteries of slavery in the South.

More champions of freedom were constantly elected to Congress. After John P. Hale had stood alone for some years in the Senate, he was reinforced by Salmon P. Chase, who was elected in 1849 from Ohio; by William H. Seward from New York in 1850; by Charles Sumner in 1851, and Henry Wilson in 1854. Other strong men were added to the Senate, like Benj. F. Wade, in 1851. "Is it not hard," asked Mr. Badger of North Carolina, during the debate on the Kansas-Nebraska bill, "if I should emigrate to Kansas, that I should be forbidden to take my old mammy" (slave-nurse) "along with me?" "The Senator entirely mistakes our position," responded Mr. Wade, "We have not the least objection to the Senator's migrating to Kansas, and taking his old mammy with him. We only insist that he shall not be permitted to sell her, after he has taken her there."

In the House of Representatives, a strong body of determined anti-slavery men gradually collected. A leader among them was Joshua R. Giddings, of Ohio, one who never feared the face of man, and so devoted to the cause of liberty that he seized every opportunity of bearding the lion in his den. With him were associated at one time John Gorham Palfrey of Massachusetts, Horace Mann of Illinois, a brother of the murdered Lovejoy, and other men of the same sterling quality.

Meantime Mr. Garrison and his friends were showing increased activity, and were using powerful motives outside of all politics, and which appealed only to the reason and conscience. At the same time there was a steady increase of the political party opposed to slavery. When in 1856 General Fremont received over a million votes, it indicated what was coming four years later when Lincoln was elected President. And the South well understood that it was as certain as anything could be, that the anti-slavery principle was to triumph eventually, as it did in Lincoln's election. This determined the Slave States to dissolve the Union by seceding from it. It was a long time before the North could be made to believe that the South was in earnest in this. I remember that Wendell Phillips used to laugh at the idea. He said it was like a set of paupers in a poor-house saying that they were going to dissolve their union with the town. He thought it was rather brag and bluster than a sincere purpose. The slaveholders, on the other hand, thought the North would never fight. They were sure, as one of their orators said directly after the organization of the Confederacy, that in fifty days the flag of the Confederacy would float over Washington, and in a few more weeks over Faneuil Hall in Boston !

As we look back now on this act of secession, it illustrates what has often been shown in history, the truth of the old proverb : "Whom God wishes to destroy, he first makes mad." It was madness in the slave-power to give up all they had gained. They held the government of the country in their hands. Before Alexander H. Stephens accepted the vice-presidency of the Southern Confederacy, he made a speech before the State Convention of Georgia, in which he pointed out how the South had everything in its hands ; all the majorities in Congress ; more than their share of presidents, secretaries of state, judges in the Supreme Court ; and great public offices. It was throwing it all away to secede. They had on their side the Democratic party. The northern Democrats were politically subservient to the slave-power, but this power deliberately broke down this party by insisting on the protection of slavery in the territories by the Federal Government. Douglas had gone so far as to accept the principle of "Squatter-sovereignty," which had a Democratic sound, and which left the people themselves to decide in every place what their institutions should be. But when the southern leaders insisted that he should turn squarely round, and maintain that the people of a territory should not decide, but that their institutions should be decided for them ; that they should be obliged to admit slavery, and that the Federal Government should enforce this obligation, it was evident that neither Mr. Douglas nor his supporters could take that step. Therefore, because the Democratic party was unwilling to go all lengths with them, the slaveholders were willing to break down its power.

What did the Republican party contend for ? Only this : that slavery should not be permitted to go into the territories where it did not already exist. Henry Clay had said over and over again, that, by his consent, no foot of soil then free from slavery should ever support a slave ; and that was all that the Republican party demanded in electing Lincoln. They had declared that they did not believe Congress had any power to interfere with the institution of slavery in the slave states, The Southerners had secured the passage of the Fugitive Slave Law. It was in full operation and declared by the U. S. Supreme Court to be Constitutional. They had the immense terri-

ritory of Texas to fill with slaves, and the promise
that four more states should be cut out of it from
which to make slave states. The state of Texas contains 273,000 square miles, an amount of territory
equal to the whole of New England, added to New
York, Pennsylvania, Maryland, Delaware, New Jersey
and Virginia. They had all this territory to over-
spread with slavery, and the Republican party made
no opposition to it. But made confident by continued
success, animated by a haughty contempt of the
North, thinking that the people of the Free States
were so peaceful and devoted to money-making, and
so much in love with trade and commerce that they
would never resist secession ; believing that " Cotton
was King," and that they could have an alliance with
foreign powers whenever they wished it, they determined to form a great slaveholding empire. Then I
think there was another reason which made them
secede. Notwithstanding their assertion that slavery
was right, there was a constant disturbance of conscience coming to them by being compelled to hear
anti-slavery doctrines. As long as they were in relation with the North they could not wholly escape it.
They imagined, if they separated from the North,
they could shut out all this, and that these obnoxious
truths might be prevented from filling their ears.
Their consciences were in an irritable state and they
wanted quiet.

Therefore, in the Democratic Convention in 1860, the Representatives of the Slave States insisted on the Federal protection of slavery in all the territories as a *sine qua non.* Because Douglas could not agree to this suicidal proposition, they seceded from the Convention in which he had the majority, and held one of their own, in which they nominated John C. Breckenridge for President.

We see how the demands of the slave-power had steadily increased. At first the slaveholders admitted that slavery was bad and wrong, but they believed it would be gradually abolished. That was the doctrine held by Jefferson and the Revolutionary Fathers. Then they said that slavery must be maintained for the present wherever it exists, but ought not to be extended to the territories. That was the view held at the time of the Dane ordinance. It excluded slavery from all territory north of the Ohio. Next, the slaveholders demanded that slavery should share the territories, equally with freedom. That was the ground taken in 1820, at the time of the Missouri Compromise. Then they maintained that slavery should not be shut out of any of the territories, but the question should be decided by the people themselves. That was the ground taken at the time of the passage of the Kansas-Nebraska bill, under the lead of Douglas. Finally, the slaveholders declared that slavery was right, and in accordance with Christianity; that it was the only foundation of freedom and of the Republic; that it must therefore be pro. tected by law, not only in the Slave States, but in every part of the country.

When it became evident that there was danger of Southern Secession, there was for a time no little probability that for the sake of union, these last demands would also be granted to them. There was danger that more concessions would be offered to induce them to remain, and that the conscience of the North would submit altogether to their claims. Horace Greeley says, in his history, that "those who had reduced servility to a science demanded that the North should make new concessions and prostrations and abasements.

The New York *Herald* declared that the South had the right to secede, and that New York City, New Jersey, and probably Connecticut would go too. The New York *Tribune* declared that journal would resist all coercive attempts to keep the South in the Union; for the right to secede, though a revolutionary right, was a real one. The ground was taken by a great many anti-slavery men, who would have preferred to have the South become an independent State, rather than have more concessions made to them. This was the opinion which I myself expressed in the pamphlet which I published at the time called "Secession, Concession, or Self-Possession."

sent to the penitentiary. " Sir," said Mr. Adams, " the only answer I make to such a threat from that gentleman, is to invite him, when he returns to his constituents, to study a little the first principles of civil liberty." He then called on a gentleman from the slave States to say, how many of them indorsed that sentiment. " I do not," said Mr. Underwood of Kentucky. " I do not," said Mr. Wise of Virginia. Mr. Thompson was compelled to attempt another explanation, and said he meant that, in *South Carolina*, any member of the Legislature who should present a petition from slaves, could be indicted. " Then," replied Mr. Adams, and this produced a great sensation, " if it is the law of South Carolina that members of her Legislature may be indicted by juries for words spoken in debate, God Almighty receive my thanks that I am not a Citizen of South Carolina."

Mr. Adams ended his speech by declaring that the honor of the House of Representatives was always regarded by him as a sacred sentiment, and that he would feel a censure from that House as the heaviest misfortune of a long life, checkered as it had been by many vicissitudes.*

When Mr. Adams began his defence, not only was a large majority of the House opposed to his course,

---

* He added that if the House wished to know what the paper was he would send it to the Speaker's desk. It proved to be a petition purporting to be from slaves, asking that John Quincy Adams be expelled from Congress.

who believed that almost anything could be done by skilful management. He who originated the phrase, "Irrepressible conflict," seemed to have forgotten that there was any conflict of principles which must continue its course regardless of politicians. There was a great meeting held in Ohio, in December, 1860, for pacifying the South, at which resolutions were passed saying that anti-slavery discussion at the North should be frowned down ; that slavery need not be excluded from the territories ; and that no one must meddle with the institutions of the Slave States.

About the same time George William Curtis having made an engagement to lecture in Philadelphia, on the "Policy of Honesty," was prevented from speaking on the ground that there would probably be a riot if he did.

Under these circumstances was the 36th Congress assembled in December, 1860. Buchanan was still President. He said in his last message that a State could not be coerced, and argued that he had no right to prevent the Slave States from seceding. He had been elected President for the purpose, as the Constitution declared, of seeing that the laws should be faithfully executed, and he declined to execute them at the South. Judge Black, Mr. Buchanan's Attorney-General, argued to the same effect. He asserted the impotence of the United States to maintain its own existence.

Congress appointed a committee to see how these
seceders could be conciliated; but they did not wish
to be conciliated. They were in earnest in their conviction that their safety was in secession, and that
only by a dissolution of the Union, and the formation
of a Southern Confederacy, could the system of chat-
tel slavery be maintained.

Mr. Iverson, of Georgia, said, "they meant to secede, and nothing Congress could do would prevent
them. There would be no war." He compared
Northerners to a "switched dog. A Southern Confederacy would soon be formed, and would be the
most successful government in the world, able to resist any force."

Mr John J. Crittenden, of Kentucky, proposed a
series of resolutions virtually surrendering to the
slaveholders all they had ever asked for.

Mr. Clark, of Rhode Island, offered a resolution to
the effect that no compromise or concession was necessary, and that the Constitution as it stood was suffi-
cient, and ought to be enforced.

In a committee of thirteen, appointed to see what
could be done to prevent secession, Mr. Seward moved
the following resolution: "No amendment shall be
made to the Constitution which will give Congress
power over slavery in the States."

When, therefore, we read the history of these few
months from the election of Lincoln to the assault on

Fort Sumter, we shall see that the great danger of the hour was that the North, for the sake of peace, would yield up everything to slavery, and then call this also a compromise.

Governor Seymour, of New York, said, at an immense Democratic convention at Albany : "The only question is, shall we have a compromise after a war, or without a war ? "

A peace conference was called and held in Washington and adopted a series of resolutions, which, however, was voted down in the United States Senate.

The compromise of 1850 having proved to be a wall so feebly built that it had already fallen down, it was now proposed to daub it with a little more untempered mortar. This, as Lowell said, was attempting " to coax an earthquake with a bun."

The secession of the Southern States then began :

South Carolina, seceded Dec. 20, 1860.
Georgia,   "  Jan. 19, 1861.
Mississippi,  "  Jan. 7, "
Florida,   "  Jan. 10, "
Louisiana,  "  Jan. 25, "
Texas,    "  Feb. 1, "
North Carolina, "  May 21, "
Tennessee,  "  June 26, "
Virginia,   "  Apr. 17, "

Kentucky tried to secede, but failed,.Maryland and and Missouri also remained in the Union, though containing a large number in full sympathy with secession.

The Confederate Government was formed, by the choice of Jefferson Davis as President, February 9, 1861.

Without waiting for any action at the North, the United States forts, thirty in all, were seized by the Confederates.

Fort Moultrie and Castle Pinckney, South Carolina, on December, 1860.

Fort Sumter surrendered April 13, 1861.

Fort Pulaski, Mount Jackson and the United States Arsenal, in Georgia, were seized January, 1861.

The Arsenal at Augusta followed.

The Florida Navy Yards and three forts in Florida were seized in January, 1861.

Fort Morgan in Alabama and the Mount Vernon Arsenal also fell.

Immense quantities of arms, ammunition, e*c., were seized by the Confederacy, in all the Southern States. Thirty forts, with 3000 guns, thus fell into their hands.

But when the first gun was fired at Fort Sumter a wonderful result took place at the North; a result which no one had foreseen. We ourselves, in the North, did not know what a love for the country there was in the hearts of the people. The Southern people had not the remotest idea that the North would attempt to resist them. But when Fort Sumter was attacked, a flame of fire seemed run through the whole North, and all parties were united to resist this assault upon the national flag. There was no more talk of any compromises with the South. Lincoln issued a proclamation calling for 75,000 troops, and more troops were offered than the Government was willing to accept; and so the civil war began. A month before that gun was fired at Sumter there were many parts of New York where it would have been dangerous for any anti-secession man to express his sentiments; the next day after, it would have been dangerous for anybody to have said a word in favor of secession, even in the worst parts of that city.

Who that lived in that time can ever forget those memorable days? Who can forget the immense excitements, the expectations, the disappointments, the trials, the great sorrows, the tragedies, the hopes and fears, the struggles, the devotion, the numerous forms of generous effort which were displayed at the North? Who that lived in such hours can forget what it is to live in a nation the whole heart and soul of which are devoted to generous and patriotic purposes, among men and women who are forgetting private interests, money-making, everything but saving the country?

No doubt there were people who made money out

of the war, and who were selfish, but that was not the spirit of the land. The feeling of most Northern men was that the Union must be saved at all hazards and at every sacrifice. They said, "if the Union goes, everything goes. It will be ruin to every interest. We may as well sacrifice all we have to save the country, for unless it is preserved, nothing we have will be of any value." This conviction was expressed by Judge Rockwood Hoar, who said to me at the beginning of the contest: "I suppose that the people of the Northern States have made up their minds that they will not give up a single shovelful of sand from the southern cape of Florida, nor a single paralytic negro from the rice-swamps of South Carolina."

## CHAPTER VII.

### THE CIVIL WAR AND ITS CONSEQUENCES.

" The roll of drums and the bugle's wailing,
 Vex the air of our vales no more;
The spear is beaten to hooks of pruning,
 The share is the sword the soldier wore.

" Sing soft, sing low, our lowland river,
 Under thy banks of laurel bloom,
Softly and sweet, as the hour becometh,
 Sing us the songs of peace and home."

        WHITTIER.

IN this story of the anti-slavery conflict, we have not been able to keep to any strict chronological order, but have preferred to hold mainly the succession of subjects. We, therefore, have now to go back to the time before the rebellion, and examine some points of interest which preceded it.

We must first speak of Abraham Lincoln, the man providentially raised up to be the saviour of the Union and the emancipator of the slaves. No such place has been occupied in modern history as he was called to fill. Singularly fitted by his character and experience for his great work, his whole life seemed to have been a preparation for it. We needed a man in that trying

hour who should be prudent but decided, cautious but
firm—a man of supreme good sense ; a conscientious
man, but no enthusiast or fanatic.   We needed one
around whom the whole loyal people could unite;
therefore, one against whom no prejudices existed,
and not an extreme partisan of any creed.   The Northern people were broken into many parties.   There
was New England, strongly anti-slavery and Republican ; the Middle States leaning to the Democratic
party, and filled with men who hated abolition ; the
Border States just on the verge of secession, and only
to be kept in the Union by a firm, yet kind, hand.
There were Douglas men, Bell and Everett men, Webster Whigs ; and men of influence like Vallandigham,
ex-President Pierce and Fernando Wood, whose sym-
pathies were with the rebels.   An anti-slavery man
would have made a large part of the Union men indifferent and neutral.   An old-fashioned Whig would
have killed the enthusiasm of the anti-slavery North.
Although at the beginning of the war, and for a long
time after the beginning, no steps were taken by the Gov
ernment toward the emancipation of the slaves, though
General Fremont's proclamation of emancipation in
Missouri was modified by the President so as to make
it inoperative, and though General Hunter's emancipation order in the South was also annulled by Lincoln, yet the anti-slavery men, though grieved, still ad-
hered to him.   They knew that he was an enemy to

slavery, and they believed that the progress of events
would certainly bring the end of that institution
through his means. They, as well as Lincoln, knew
how to "bide their time." Lincoln was patient,
hopeful, determined, wise. He was one of the people,
and knew them well. He had that instinct of humanity which alone enables a man to measure public sentiment. Trained in poverty and hardship, he was not
easily discouraged by difficulties. With a heart tender
as that of a woman, he had a cool, calm brain. At the
root of all was "the strong-siding champion, conscience." Whatever might happen, in evil report or
good report, he was determined to do his duty, and he
did it to the end. A sad man, on whom the burden
of responsibility weighed heavily, his quick, rugged
humor furnished him a little distraction and relief.

Some hitherto unpublished anecdotes of Lincoln's
early life in Springfield, throwing light on his character,
were communicated to me by one of my old Kentucky
friends, who was also one of the oldest friends of Lincoln. I have spoken before of Judge Speed, the Kentucky farmer, who, though a slaveholder, was an utter
unbeliever in slavery, and whose slaves were set free
by his children at his death. One of his sons, named
Joshua, went, while quite young, to Springfield, Illinois, and there kept a country shop. Abraham Lincoln, who had recently opened his lawyer's office in
the town, came into the store one day, and said, "Mr.

Speed, I have put a bedstead in my back office, and now
I want the *furniture* of the bed—a mattrass, pillows,
blankets and sheets.   I cannot pay you now, but suppose I can when the next term of court is held."
Speed, who knew him somewhat, told him the price,
but added, " Mr. Lincoln, I have a large room and a
large bed above my shop ; if you like, you can come
and stay there with me."   " How do I get there ? "
asked Lincoln ; and mounting the staircase, with his
saddlebags, deposited them in the corner of the room,
and coming down again, said, " Mr. Speed, I have
moved in."

They lived together thus for five years, and became
warm friends.   When Lincoln was President, he selected a brother of Joshua, James Speed, who was an
excellent lawyer, and also possessing the fine integrity
of the family, as his Attorney-General.

I spent a summer afternoon with Joshua Speed, at
his late residence in Kentucky, and he told me many
anecdotes showing some of the early traits of Lincoln's
character.   During all the time he knew him, he said
that Lincoln was devoted to his profession—conscientious, truthful, honorable.   He indulged in none of the
dissipations, still less in the vices, all too common in
those days.   He did not drink, and was temperate in
all things.   Of his interest in the law, the following is
an illustration :—" He once was retained in a case in
which the question at issue concerned the boundary of

a piece of land on the prairie. Now, as there are no trees nor stones on the prairie, the surveyors were in the habit of fixing the corners of the lots by shovelling up a little mound of earth. But it seemed that the prairie squirrel, there called a gopher, built a somewhat similar mound over his house. The question then was whether, in this particular instance, the mound at the corner had been put up by the surveyor or by the gopher. Lincoln sent to New York to get books on natural history, and studied in them the habits of the little animal. When the trial came, he went into court and explained to the judge and jury the difference between the surveyor's mound and that raised by the gopher. The latter being anxious for the comfort of his small family below, was careful to beat down the roof firmly, and make it slope up to a point in the middle, so that the rain might run off. The surveyor, less anxious, was apt to leave his mound with a flat or hollow top. After the trial was over, the judge, who happened in this instance to be Lincoln's future rival, Stephen A. Douglas, went to Lincoln's office, and found him, with his books of natural history, still studying the habits of these animals. He had no more practical need of the knowledge, but had become interested in the subject, and so went on with the study. Judge Douglas and Lincoln spent the evening over these books, little thinking of the future time when their mutual struggles would shake the country, and make one of them the President of the United States.

Sunday morning, April 14th, 1861, Fort Sumter was surrendered by Major Anderson to the chivalry of South Carolina. Lincoln had then been President a little more than a month. On the 15th he issued his proclamation calling for seventy-five thousand troops to enforce the laws in the States in insurrection. The war then began, which ended four years after by the surrender of Lee's army, April 9th, 1865.

At first everything in this war seemed to go against the North. The South had every advantage. They had secured the munitions of war, and had dispersed the U, S. troops to the farthest parts of the west and southwest. The Union had no navy, no army, and had an empty treasury. The Government had to borrow of the New York banks a few million dollars to commence operations. The Southerners had been brought up to the use of weapons ; the Northerners had not. The Southern men were quite accustomed to fight ; they lived in a permanent condition of war, and therefore it was natural enough, though it seemed melancholy, that we should be defeated in our first battles. Those were very gloomy times for Union men. We looked abroad for sympathy, but we did not find it. We had hoped that the influence of England would be on our side, as it had made such strong anti-slavery professions, but the leading men there were all opposed to us.   The aristocracy, the army and navy, the church and literary men, all took sides with the slaveholders, and there were only on our side a few men like John Bright, Richard Cobden, Goldwin Smith, J. Stuart Mill, and the laboring class among the people.   With that instinct, deeper than reason and larger than knowledge, that led the common people to hear Christ gladly, while the wise and prudent refused to listen to him, the common laborers in the mills of Lancashire, the manufacturing classes, though depending on cotton for their daily bread, nevertheless refused to echo the public sentiment against the Union.   They stood by it to the last, even though many were on the point of starvation in consequence of their position.

We sent to England as our ambassador, a man who was singularly well fitted to be our representative, Mr. Charles Francis Adams.   He was calm, cool, prudent, wise, very determined, very inflexible—like his father before him.   He had a very hard time living in the midst of all this sentiment in favor of the Confederacy, but he held his own against it.   When Lord Russell refused to stop the building of rams for the Confederates, Mr. Adams simply said, " Of course, your lordship is aware that this is war."   Orders were then given by Lord Russell to suspend the building of these Confederate rams.   Lord Russell had said that " Jefferson Davis had created a nation."   Most Englishmen were quite certain that the North could never conquer the South. They called it a war of ambition on the part of the North, and said we ought to let the South go. The English aristocracy, literary men and merchants wished to see our nation divided and weakened. Their motive was, that they found the United States growing into too-powerful a nation; it was as suming altogether too much importance, and it would be extremely satisfactory to have it broken into two or three divisions. For all this there came the judgment, when England was not only obliged to pay for the destruction caused by these Confederate cruisers that she had allowed to be built in her ports to destroy American shipping, but to admit that she had done wrong in letting them go.

When the great uprising of the Northern people came, there was seen in the Northern States "the might that slumbers in a freeman's arm." The Whig party, led by such men as Webster and Clay, and the Democrats of the North under their own great leaders, had been taught to believe in the importance of the Union and the Constitution. And the Republican party, which had grown up under the teaching of the political and non-political sections of their anti-slavery teachers, had been taught to believe that the great danger to the country, was from slavery. When secession came it struck a blow at both these great sentiments. It attacked the national union, and it attacked it in behalf of slavery and its extension. It thus struck a blow at the same time at the Union sentiment and the anti-slavery sentiment, and the Northern States united as one man against secession.

Immense armies were speedily improvised. Fifty days after the battle of Bull Run, when the army of the Potomac had been apparently demoralized, another army of a hundred thousand men was collected in Washington, under McClellan, and were organized by him into a highly disciplined body of troops. A blockade of the Southern States was declared. Abroad this was thought to be utterly impracticable, but the Southern coast for fifteen hundred miles was soon watched and guarded. It is true that many blockade runners got through, but our blockade was admitted to be, on the whole efficient.

There had never been in this country any truly organized banking system. Salmon P. Chase, Secretary of the Treasury, has the credit of having first established the National banking system, which certainly has proved from that day to this a vastly better one than any that had before existed in this country. Down to that time, exchange was to be paid on the notes of one state in another, and there were continual failures of the state banks all over the country. But our new banks were even better than the old United States Bank under Nicholas Biddle.

The arsenals in the country were soon at work turning out thousands of guns and rifles every day.

And very soon, by the foresight and eloquence of Henry W. Bellows, the Sanitary Commission was in full operation. This was a new gift to mankind' showing how the horrors of war could be soothed and its evils be alleviated by the power of kind, generous, wise and faithful care on the part of those at home for those who were at the front. The best women of the land joined the army as nurses. They were to be found in all the hospitals ; at work, everywhere, on the field, and at home providing comforts for the soldiers. I recollect, one Sunday, when news came that there had been a battle, and that a quantity of goods were wanted for the comfort of the soldiers. It was advertised that they might be sent to a place opposite the Tremont House, in Boston. The whole of that sidewalk, on Sunday afternoon was filled with boxes from many towns around, sent in for that purpose.

After two or three years the largest, best disciplined, best commanded army the world has ever seen had been organized, composed of "those bayonets which could not only fight but also think." Our generals were at first inexperienced, but they became wise and skilful, until we had such men as Grant, Sherman, Sheridan, Thomas, Burnside, Hooker, and Meade at the head of our armies.

Meantime the nation was ready to give all, bear all and do all. Every prophecy of evil made concerning it failed. It had been said that no nation could carry on a civil war and at the same time allow free speech and a free press. We did both. The newspapers at the North which were favorable to the Confederates continued to be printed, and were allowed to say what they thought. Meetings were held to denounce the war, conventions were called to oppose the war and the people who sat in them were allowed full freedom to speak. It was said that when Mason and Slidell were taken and there was such an outbreak of glad enthusiasm at the North, that the American people would never consent to their being given up to England. When the nation found that this was the necessary thing to do, no opposition was made to it anywhere. It took place in silence. It was said that a free election of a President was not possible in the midst of such a war ; but when Lincoln's four years of service expired, another election took place, which was carried through as though it had been in the midst of profound peace.

It was said that a nation spending two million dollars a day in war expenses would soon become a bankrupt. At one time the paper money of the United States had depreciated immensely ; nevertheless we were never bankrupt. We never repudiated our debts. It was said that if the South was conquered in the field, it would carry on a perpetual guerrilla warfare. But when Lee and Johnson surrendered, the war came to an end. It was said that reconstruction would be impossible ; that the Southern States were so hostile to the North that they would never come back ; but we very soon saw them willingly taking their places in the Union, consenting to alter their Constitutions to abolish slavery. We have seen a new prosperity, a new contentment come over the whole land. It was said that this enormous debt could never be paid off, but about half of it has already been paid. It was said that the immense Northern army would never consent to be disbanded, but would reduce the country under military control ; but as soon as the war was over the army melted away and disappeared ; glad to return to private life and to take up its old occupations. It was said that if the negroes were emancipated, they would not work, but would gradually die out ; but at present the fear expressed is that they are increasing so rapidly that they will finally drive out the white people from the Southern States.

What gave this power to the people of the Union ? Free schools, free churches, a free press, popular institutions. The people of the country knew that it was *their* country ; that it belonged to them ; that they had a right to make of it anything they chose, to do anwhing they wished with it. They felt the

immense benefit rendered to them by these free institutions. They had been educated by free schools
to understand these principles ; they had been taught
in free churches to make sacrifices for the general
good. They knew that the country was their common country ; and that it must be defended and preserved for the common welfare.

There were many providential circumstances to be
noticed in those times. A friend of mine once said
to me during the war, " Mr. Clarke, it does not now
require any faith to see the presence of a divine Providence in our affairs ; it only requires common
sense."

It was a providential thing that we had such a man
as Abraham Lincoln for President. If we had had a
man who was more satisfactory to the abolitionist
and anti-slavery party, he would not have united the
whole nation. At any rate he would not have induced the Border States to remain in the Union. On
the other hand, if we had had a man opposed to the
anti-slavery movement, neither would he have united
the nation. As it was, we had a man who in heart
and conviction was opposed to slavery, but whose
main object was to save the Union. He said on one
occasion, " If the Union can be best saved by emancipating all the slaves, I am willing to emancipate
them all. If it can be best saved by emancipating a
part, I am ready to emancipate a part. And if it can

be best saved by not emancipating any, I will emancipate none." He did not go too fast, and yet he kept moving on. He knew the people. Every great statesman has been able to divine what the people need and want. I remember hearing Gov. Andrew tell a story of Andrew Jackson. He was advised that some measure which he favored was not Democratic. " I don't want any one to tell me what is Democratic," he cried ; "if I want to know what is Democratic, I ask old Andrew Jackson ; *he* knows what is Democratic if no one else does. He is a Democrat if any one is."

Mr. Lincoln had no military knowledge. Jefferson Davis was an educated soldier. Mr. Lincoln was at first obliged to put himself entirely in the hands of General Scott and other generals, and do as they said. When Gen. McClellan still lingered so long after the army had been prepared, and found it so difficult to move forward, Mr. Lincoln said to one of his friends, "I wonder whether McClellan means to do anything. If not I should like to *borrow* the army of him for a week or two. He took an immense interest in everything connected with the war, and he had that faculty which enables a man to make use of men different from himself. He could see the good in men of all sorts ; in Mr. Seward, for example, who was a politician ; in Sumner, a scholar and thinker. They both were great friends of Lincoln. He was also very fond of Stanton, who opposed Lincoln in almost everything. He made use of them all for the purposes of the national life.

So though Lincoln was thought to be slow at first, and though he was distrusted by many, he grew in the love and esteem of the whole nation, and also in real strength and power. At last he felt himself able to decide for himself, on the measures needed at the hour, forming his own conclusions, and acting decidedly upon them. No one ever could take more to heart than Lincoln did the terrible burdens of the war. Some of our generals seemed to act as though they were going through a routine and needed not to trouble themselves much about their work. Not so with Lincoln. On him this awful struggle rested as a dreadful weight, and he would have been crushed but for three things. He had faith in the justice of God. He was a profoundly religious man at heart, though without any religious formality or cant. He had a strong faith also in free institutions, and was sure that they must ultimately triumph. Then he had a sense of humor and social sympathy which were often a help to him in the hours of greatest calamity. When he told his Cabinet that he had decided on issuing the Proclamation of Emancipation, he said that he had been waiting for the right time to come, and he was sure that the time had arrived. He had watched the sentiment of the people, and he was satisfied that the whole nation was prepared for this step. Then he added in a low voice, heard only by one person, "When Lee was driven out of Maryland I promised my God that I would abolish slavery."

When Gen. McClellan's army was defeated in the Peninsula, Lincoln said that he was about as inconsolable as any man could be and live.

Lincoln's humanity and sympathy were very great. There was a story told me by Mr. James Speed, his attorney-general, to this effect. One day when he met Mr. Lincoln to consult him on some point, the officer on guard came in and said, "Your excellency, there is a poor woman outside crying. She has been there two or three days, asking if she cannot see you." "Let here come in," said Lincoln. She came in and said, "Oh, Mr. President, I have three sons in the army. I am a widow. I had one son at home, and now he is dead. Won't you lend me one of my sons to carry on my farm and help support me." "Well,' said Lincoln, "I have three children; it does seem as though you ought to have one. Where is your son?" "Oh, sir, he is with the army at Fredericksburg." "What is his name, and with what command is he?" When he had learned these facts he sat down and wrote an order for his discharge. She blessed him and took the paper and was going out when Lincoln said, where are you going?" "Please, sir, I am going directly to Fredericksburg to get my son."

" How do you expect to get through the lines to find him ? " " The Lord will take care of that, so long as I have your paper." " I do not know," said Lincoln, " whether it is necessary to trouble the Lord about it ; I can attend to that myself." So he sat down and wrote an order passing her through the lines and directing every one to give her the help she needed.

A gentleman who was in the office of Secretary Stanton told me that when any soldier had committed an offence for which he was sentenced to death by the Court Martial, the sentence was never executed till the proceedings of the Court had been revised both by Stanton and Lincoln. Then it almost always happened that Lincoln wished to commute, and Stanton to execute the sentence. Stanton once said, " Mr. President, you think you will be doing an act of mercy in pardoning this man " (who had disobeyed orders, deserted in battle, or committed some outrage on peaceful citizens), " it is not mercy, it is cruelty. For every such rascal pardoned, a hundred good and honest soldiers will be killed." " It may be so," replied Lincoln ; " but then that is only a possibility ; but if I let this man be shot, it will be a certainty that I have allowed the death of one soldier."

It is said that on one occasion, when it was thought that it was absolutely necessary that there should be a new Surgeon-General appointed, and Dr. Bellows was asked to go to Washington to urge the appointment of Dr. Hammond, he went, and had an inter-view with Lincoln, whom he found signing papers.

"Go on," said Lincoln, "I can hear you while I write." So Dr. Bellows made his plea with his usual energy. Lincoln kept signing his papers. At last, after Bellows had got through, and stopped, Lincoln said, "I like to hear you talk, Doctor; but I rather think Hammond has been appointed, at least a week ago." "Is that so?" asked Dr. Bellows. "Yes, that is so; but I thought I would like to hear your oration."

He was a sad-eyed, earnest, wise, kind man, but this fondness for fun perhaps saved his life more than once. He was once called upon to address a crowd from the window of a hotel. He was tall, and his wife, who was very short, was standing at the window with him. The whole speech was in these words: "My friends, here am I, and here is Mrs. Lincoln. That is the long and the short of the whole matter."

The best description that has ever been given of him was that of James Russell Lowell, in his Com-memoration Ode at Cambridge:

> Nature, they say, doth dote,
>   And cannot make a man,
>   Save on some worn-out plan,
> Repeating us by rote.
> For him her Old World moulds aside she threw,
>   And, choosing sweet clay from the breast
>   Of the unexhausted west,
> With stuff untainted shaped a hero new,

Wise, zealous in the strength of God, and true.
How beautiful to see
  Once more, a shepherd of mankind, indeed,
  Who loved his charge, but never loved to lead ;
One whose meek flock the people joyed to be. . . .
They knew that outward grace is dust ;
They could not choose, but trust
  In that sure-footed mind's unfaltering skill,
  And supple-tempered will,
That bent, like perfect steel, to spring again and thrust
Great captains, with their guns and drums,
  Disturb our judgment for the hour ;
But, at last, silence comes;
  These all are gone, and standing like a tower,
Our children shall behold his fame—
  The kindly, earnest, brave, foreseeing man,
Sagacious, patient, dreading praise, not blame ;
  New birth of our new soil—the first American."

In February, 1862, an assault was made by the
Federal troops on Fort Henry in Tennessee. This
was one of the first Federal successes of the war. At
that time the gunboats which Fremont had ordered
to be built came into most efficient use. The Government had refused to accept these boats ; and it is
said that the contractors, having turned them over to
the Government, and the Government not being
willing to accept them, they lay three days at the
Cairo landing without any owner at all. There were
twelve of these armored gunboats under Flag Officer
Foote, which went up the Tennessee river in order to
break the Confederate lines. The Confederates had
established a line of posts across the country to prevent the Union army from getting down through
Kentucky. General Grant commanded the Union

troops, and Foote the gunboats. They captured Fort
Henry in two hours, and then attacked Fort Donald-
son, on the Cumberland river. In the last, 20,000
men were in garrison, under Pillow and Floyd, of
whom 13,500 surrendered to Grant. This success
gave great confidence to the North, and showed that
some of our commanders believed in carrying on the
war in earnest,

One of the discouragements of the Northern people
was, that they thought justly or otherwise, that some
of the generals in command had no faith in the war;
no expectation of success ; no sympathy with the
cause for which they fought. The Northern people
gave their lives and their fortunes for union and
freedom, and it was a bitter thought that those in
command sometimes were not in earnest in this great
cause.

But, however that might be with the army, no one
doubted the devoted courage and chivalry of the
naval commanders. With what science and what
calm skill did the Union fleet steam past the forts at
Hitton Head, silencing their batteries, and putting the
United States in possession of the sea-islands of
Georgia and South Carolina. How thrilling was the
description of the passage by Farragut, of the Confederate forts on the Mississippi, which resulted in the
taking of New Orleans ; and his daring entrance into
Mobile harbor, in spite of forts, ships and torpedoes !

The defences of New Orleans consisted of a fort on each side the river, together with a heavy boom across the stream, bound with chains and anchored ; a fleet of war steamers behind it, together with five ships. This defence was thought to make the city impregnable. The attack on the forts began with Porter's mortar fleet of 21 schooners, each carrying a mortar which threw a shell weighing two hundred pounds. With these, Admiral Porter bombarded Forts Philip and Jackson, during six days. Then Farragut, on the night of April 23d, 1862, ran past them with his fleet of eighteen vessels, and broke the boom. Having passed the forts he encountered the Confederate vessels. The Cayuga was attacked by sixteen, and though struck forty-two times, took three of them. The Varuna drove three ashore, and sank a fourth, and then ran ashore herself and sank. In an hour and a half the forts were passed, and the Confederate fleet taken or sunk. New Orleans then surrendered to General Butler and the Union army.

How exciting was the account of the battle between the Merrimac and the Monitor. The United States war-ship Merrimac, taken by the Confederates at Norfolk, had been turned by them into a great iron-clad. At that time little was known of the power of iron-clad vessels. The Merrimac was the first floating steam battery ; and it demonstrated that a new ele-

ment had appeared in naval warfare. It had been for
some time rumored that she was in preparation. On
March 8th, 1862, she was seen moving down the James
river, looking like a black ark of iron. She approached
the United States vessels lying in the bay. The
Merrimac ran at the United States frigate Cumberland, and rammed it with its powerful beak, and with a
tremendous blow laid open half the side of the vessel,
which, with all aboard, and with her flag flying, went
down, in 54 feet of water.*

The Merrimac then destroyed the United States
frigate Congress in a few minutes, notwithstanding
the repeated broadsides poured at the ironclad from
its heavy batteries. The shot glanced off harmless
from her iron roof, like hail from a housetop. Having
accomplished so easily the destruction of two of the
best war vessels of the Union, the Confederate iron-
clad turned to another. The Minnesota, the most
powerful vessel in the service, was lying at anchor, or
aground, when the Confederate went to attack her.
One or two broadsides were delivered on either side,
when the commanding officer of the Confederate
vessel, fearing to get aground himself, turned and went
back to Norfolk.

All that night the telegrams sent the terrible news
through the North. This impregnable vessel would, no

* In 1854, on my way to Grant's headquarters. I saw the topmast
still out of water.

doubt, return the next day, and easily destroy the Minnesota. What then? Why should she not, after taking Fortress Monroe, enter any of our harbors, and demolish, or capture, New York or Boston. The wildest apprehension prevailed wherever the news went. But a power had been providentially prepared to put an end to her career of terror.

Mr. Erricson, an eminent engineer and inventor, had foreseen with the intuition of genius, the change which must take place in naval warfare in consequence of the introduction of ironclads. At his own expense, and with only partial encouragement from the United States Government, he had built a small vessel. show. ing little surface above the water, plated heavily, and with a revolving tower of iron, containing one heavy gun. This vessel, the existence of which was scarcely known, had just been finished, and was towed round by a steamer to Fortress Monroe. Once or twice on the passage, she came near being lost. But she arrived in time. When the Merrimac came down the river the next morning to complete her work of destruction, this little machine which looked like a large cheese-box on the water, interposed, and pounded away with her heavy balls at every open porthole. She was too alert for her massive opponent, and finally drove it back to Norfolk, from which it never came out again.

This battle revolutionized naval warfare throughout

the world. Wooden ships were made useless, and England, France, and other countries, began to build ironclads.

January 1, 1863, came the proclamation of President Lincoln, which declared the slaves in all the rebel states to be free. That was what the Northern people had been longing for, and hoping, but were by no means sure it would ever come. Long ago, when John Quincy Adams stood alone in Congress, and when it was said that under no circumstance could the United States Government abolish slavery, he replied, " I don't agree to that. There is one state of things in which slavery can be abolished in this government. If there should be an insurrection or rebellion in the United States, it would be competent for the war-power in the hands of the President or even of any General in command, to abolish slavery."*

At this time the plan of enlisting regiments of colored troops was begun, chiefly by the urgent efforts of Governor Andrew of Massachusetts.

John Albion Andrew has been called, and justly the great war governor. We may also apply to him the words said of William Pitt. He was "the pilot that weathered the storm." A lawyer in Boston, working hard in his profession, few persons were

---

* The abolitionists, whom nothing escaped which bore on the subject of slavery, published a tract at the time, containing extracts from these declarations of J. Q. Adams, concerning the constitutional right of the war-power to abolish slavery.

aware of his great abilities until he was chosen governor of Massachusetts in 1861. He had been devoted and consistent in his anti-slavery principles from his youth. Fearless in doing and saying whatever he believed right, he was wise, kindly and tolerant of differences of opinion; though with a power of indignation which, when roused, swept everything before it. He was one of the best-tempered men I ever knew. His sagacity was like intuition. He had an immense working power, and in his office at the State House would tire out all his clerks and amanuenses, and then send them home, and continue working alone till late at night. His influence at Washington was great, and he used it to urge forward all means of putting down the rebellion. He was in constant communication with Lincoln, Stanton, Seward, Chase, the governors of the Northern States, and the Senators and Representatives of Massachusetts. On the very day of his inauguration as governor, January 1st, 1861, three months before the attack on Sumter, he sent messages to the governors of each of the New England States, assuring them that war was imminent, and that they had best begin at once to prepare for it. He himself put Massachusetts in such a state of readiness, that as soon as Lincoln's war-proclamation was issued, April 15th, he called out four regiments to go to Washington, and they were assembled the next day, April 16th, on Boston Com-

mon, every company full. The Sixth regiment left
for Washington that evening, passed through Baltimore, where some of its number were killed by the
mob, and was the first full regiment that reached
Washington. During the war Governor Andrew was
untiring, using his own private means when necessary, for public objects, and died leaving to his family
as their inheritance his great reputation and noble
character. As soon as the war was over he urged rec-
onciliation and reunion. "After a vigorous prosecution of the war," said he, in his farewell address, "let
us now devote ourselves to a vigorous prosecution of
peace."*

* The following passages are from an article in a journal reviewing
Gen. Schouler's "History of Massachusetts in the Civil War."

On the fifth of January, 1861, John Albion Andrew entered on his
duties as Governor of Massachusetts His apprehension of the approaching conflict were clearly shown in his inaugural speech. That
very night he forwarded to each of the other five New England Governors letters confidential, in which he urged the necessity of preparation for the crisis he so clearly saw impending. The next day a general order required that national salutes should be fired in the large
towns, on the approaching eighth of January, to commemorate not
only the great victory of New Orleans, but also ajor Anderson's
"·gallant conduct and wise foresight'' in taking possession of Fort
Sumter Eight days latei came General Order No. 4, calling for exact returns of all the volunteer militia, requiring that every company
should be full, and that none should be kept on the rolls who could
not, or who would not, respond to any call that might come for active
service. On the first of February the legislature put at the Governor's disposal an "emergency fund" of one hundred thousand dollars. It also appropriated twenty-five thousand dollars to provide
overcoats and equipage for two thousand men, and authorized the
Governor to organize as many companies and regiments as the public
exigency might require. Accordingly, earnest efforts were made to

Always a friend of the colored people, Governor
Andrew was unwearied in urging on the government

strengthen the militia; the overcoats were procured; a wide corre-
spondence was kept up; a cipher for secret messages was devised ; the
condition of the seaboard forts was scrutinized, and the quickest,
safest route for troops to Washington was carefully considered.    No
pains were spared in obtaining constant and reliable information from
the seat of government.

Thus, for four anxious months, things went on amid alternating
hopes and fears, and then came Sumter.    On the 15th of April a message by the wire called on Governor Andrew to send two regiments to
Washington.    Four colonels, namely, Wardrop, Packard, Jones and
Monroe, were instantly ordered to muster their regiments on Boston
Common.    On the morning of the 16th the troops began to come in—
three companies from Marblehead being first on the ground.    In the
evening of the same day the Sixth Regiment (Colonel Jones) left Boston by rail.    At the same hour on the 17th the Third Regiment
(Colonel Wardrop) embarked for Fortress Monroe and almost simul-
taneously the Fourth Regiment (Colonel Packard) having the same
destination, started on the Old Colony Railroad.    The Eighth Regiment (Colonel Monroe), after two days' detention in Boston, left on
the 18th by the Worcester road, accompanied by General Butler, who
had been appointed to command the brigade.    On Saturday, the 20th,
the Third Battalion of Rifles (Major Devens) took the cars at Worcester for the South, and the next morning the Fifth Regiment (Colonel Lawrence) started on the same road from the station in Boston.
With them went also Major Cook's Light Battery, with seventy horses
and six brass six-pounders.    Of the regiments thus forwarded during
that memorable week, the *Sixth Massachusetts* bears the high distinc-
tion of being the first to shed its blood in the great conflict, and the
first to enter Washington.

Such was the noble response of Massachusetts when the country
called on her for help.    And this community—be it ever remembered
—thus suddenly fired with patriotic ardor,—these troops which set
out so promptly for distant fields of unknown difficulty and danger,
were the peace-loving, money-getting, unwarlike "Yankees" of the
North, of whom the seceding Southerners could speak only with contempt.

How strange it seems that the generous ardor and willing service
of Massachusetts in that perilous crisis of the nation should meet with

the employment of colored troops. At last he was permitted to raise them, and send them to the front as part of the Massachusetts quota.

After many defeats of the Army of the Potomac, under McLellan, Pope, Burnside and Hooker, it was at last victorious at Gettysburg, under General Meade, July 1st, 1863 ; and on July 4th, Vicksburg was sur-rendered to General Grant. The Mississippi was thus opened through its entire course to New Orleans.

May 6th, 1864, General Sherman commenced his "march to the sea." By a series of skilful manœuvres, he had passed round the army of Johnson, who was then relieved by order of Jefferson Davis. Hood was placed in command of the Confederate army opposed to Sherman, he being believed to be more of a fight-ing man. But he proved unable to stop the progress of General Sherman, who sent back whatever he did not need by General Thomas, who was left to resist

anything but a cordial welcome at the seat of government! Early in May, 1861, ten thousand Massachusetts men had organized in com-panies, and were ready, even anxious, to enlist for the three years' service. Governor Andrew offered them to the War Department, and in repeated messages urged that they should be accepted. Days, weeks even, passed without a word of reply from the War Office. It was not till the 22nd of May that a frigid answer came from Secretary Cameron, consenting that Massachusetts should send six regiments, but strongly hinting that there was no need of so many. How Gover-nor Andrew felt in view of this strange coldness and neglect,—this evident failure to appreciate the magnitude and the dangers of the situation,—very clearly appears in his admirable letter to Montgomery Blair.

Hood. Sherman with the rest of his force marched into the heart of Georgia, cutting loose from his base of supplies, and disappearing from the knowledge of the Northern people, who did not hear for a long time anything about his movements. He had made up his mind that he could march through Georgia, although such a great army had perhaps never before been turned into a detached corps. He was satisfied that he could supply his troops from the country, and he succeeded. It was predicted that they would be destroyed, but they had an easy and cheerful march, though the Southern journals kept sending word that we should never hear of Sherman or his army again. Sherman went on, without difficulty, till, reaching the sea, he took Savannah, and caused the fall of Charleston. He then marched through South Carolina and North Carolina, till he was able to co-operate with Grant before Richmond.

Finally, Lee was defeated by utter exhaustion, after making a grand military resistance during many years, and showing all the qualities of a great general. General Grant's persistency and ability at last was crowned with success, and so ended this war of giants.

Then came the assassination of Lincoln, and the long period of reconstruction, in which a great many difficult problems were to be solved. One by one the

Southern States were re-admitted into the Union, on the condition of abolishing slavery.

Looking back now we can easily see how many things were re-admitted into the Union on the condition of abolishing slavery.

Looking back now we can easily see how many things which seemed very sad and mysterious at the time, were in reality blessings in disguise. All can now understand what a blessing it was that the North had been taught, in its schools and churches, and by its two great parties, the value of the Union. We can also recognize a providence in having Lincoln for a President. But it was also providential that the South at first had better success in the war than the Northern armies. It has been often said, and said truly, that if we had won victories at the beginning of the war, there would have been a compromise, which would have allowed slavery to continue. Our early disasters were an advantage in another way. If we had had great successes at first, and if the Southern armies had been defeated, they would have been scattered through the South, and we might have had to carry on a long guerilla warfare. How difficult that would have been, we know by the experience of Napoleon in his attempt to conquer Spain, which he could not do with an army of veterans of three hundred thousand men, under his best generals. It was an advantage to the North that the South possessed such

a splendid general in Lee. They had such confidence
in him that they put all their men into his hands, till,
when he and his army were destroyed, there were
none left to make any further resistance.

It was good for us that we were forced, almost
against our will, to use negro troops. We did it re-
luctantly, but we found they fought nobly. They
were braver even than the white troops, for they
fought often with a halter around their necks. They
knew that the slaveholders would give them no quar-
ter if they were taken prisoners. Still, while we paid
the white troops thirteen dollars a month and clothing, the colored troops received only ten dollars, and
out of that they paid about three dollars for clothing,
leaving only seven dollars, instead of thirteen, for
their pay  Gov. Andrew felt great indignation at this
unjust discrimination on account of color. He once
showed me a letter he had just written to the Massachusetts Senators, in which he requested them to
urge upon Congress and the President the great injustice done in not having the colored troops on an
equality with the white   " I will not rest," said he,
in conclusion, " until this injustice is removed. I will
not allow you any rest until it is removed. I will not
die till I have seen justice done ; or, if I should die,
and should I have any standing in the other world, I
will pursue the matter there before the throne of In-
finite Justice." I told Governor Andrew that I

was going to Washington, and that I would take the letter to Mr. Sumner and Mr Wilson, and try to see the Attorney-General. I was to preach in the House of Representatives the following Sunday, and I took occasion to describe in my sermon the character and conduct of those colored troops. I told how the Massachusetts legislature had voted that money should be taken to the colored regiments in South Carolina, so as to make up the full amount to the men for all the time they had been in the service. These troops had steadily refused to accept the ten dollars, and had gone without pay for some time. The agents of Massachusetts who carried the money explained to the troops that the State of Massachusetts, unwilling that they should serve without full pay, had sent this money as justly due to them. They were to add that Governor Andrew was anxious that they should accept it. This was done, and after the soldiers had consulted among themselves, one was appointed to reply. He said they were much obliged to the State of Massachusetts, to Governor Andrew, and to the gentlemen who had come there to bring the money, but they did not consider themselves as the troops of Massachusetts. They were now United States soldiers, and they would not take any money, not even the ten dollars offered by Government, though their families were suffering for it, until they could have what was justly their due ; meantime, they meant to do their duty just as well as if paid. When I had told that story, I said to the members of Congress before me :—" If this had been done by Greeks or Romans, an account of it would have been put into all our schoolbooks, and our children would have been taught to read it as an example of heroism. But as it is only done by colored people, we do not think much of it. Nevertheless in the sight of humanity and of history, I had rather be one of those colored soldiers, doing my duty as a man, and refusing this money till I could get justice with it, than a member of Congress, receiving my pay regularly, and sitting in my comfortable seat, and not able to muster courage to pass a law to pay those soldiers their just debt." When I said that I supposed they would be displeased ; but instead of that they applauded.

Who that was not then living can tell how, when peace came, the very air seemed full of joy, hope and content ! This feeling of the joy of returning peace, of re-established union, of the end of the great evil and danger of the nation, filled all hearts with a grateful sense of the Divine love. This was best expressed by Whittier in one of his fine lyrics, of which the following stanzas are a part :—

> " Boom, cannon, boom, to all the hills and waves!
> Clash out glad bells from every rocking steeple!
> Banners, adance in triumph ! bend your staves !

And from every mountain peak,
Let beacon fires to answering beacons speak,
Katahdin tell Monadnock, Whiteface he,
And so leap on in light from sea to sea,
Making the earth more firm and air breathe braver.
Be proud, for she is saved, and all have helped to save her,
She, that lifts up the manhood of the poor,
She of the open soul and open door,
With room about her hearth for all mankind!
The fire is dreadful in her eyes no more;
From her bold front the helm she doth unbind,
Sends all her handmaid armies back to spin,
And bids her navies, that so lately hurled
Their crashing battle, hold their thunders in,
Swimming, like birds of calm, along the unharmful shore.
No challenge sends she to the elder world,
That looked askance and hated; a light scorn
Plays o'er her mouth, as round her mighty knees
She calls her children back, and waits the morn
Of nobler day enthroned between her subject seas."

No description can convey the sense of gratitude and gladness which we had, not only because peace had come and our sufferings and trials were at an end, but because peace brought freedom and union, because the country was once more to be united, and without the blot of slavery existing in it. Slavery was ended ! That great danger and evil was gone and the South itself in a little while was glad that it was gone. A few years after the war was over I went to the Sea Islands of South Carolina, to Charleston, and Savannah, and I found scarcely a man even then who did not admit that it was the best thing for the Southern States to have slavery abolished. Though they suffered so much in the process, they would not have it back. They admitted that the colored people were working well, and making great progress. It is not too much to say that there is not one sensible man in a thousand who would have slavery back. Last winter I was told by a Boston gentleman that he had a conversation with two grand-sons of Calhoun, who was the embodiment of the pro-slavery theory. He asked how many sensible people would be glad to see slavery re-established. One re-plied, " Not a man in a hundred," and the other said, " Not one in a thousand." " Well," asked my informant, "what would your grandfather have said to that ? " " If our grandfather were now living he would say the same thing," was the reply,

Before the civil war, the cotton crop of the whole South amounted to some four millions of bales  Last year the cotton crop was seven million bales. That is the best possible proof of two important facts in re-gard to the progress of the colored people. Since the land in the cotton-growing States belongs mostly to the white people, and the labor mostly to the colored people, the great production of cotton shows, first, that the colored people are working better than they did as slaves, and secondly, that the whites and colored people are working together in peaceful relations.

The colored people also feel the need of getting an education. Every opportunity they have for going to school they eagerly seize. Old and young go to school.

Those who think themselves too old to learn, are grateful that their children can learn. I remember being told by a lady, who has been a teacher of the colored people in Port Royal, South Carolina, ever since it fell into the hands of our troops, that she one day saw an old colored woman kneeling by the side of the schoolhouse. "Why, mammy," she asked, "what are you doing there?" "Oh, missis, I'm too old for larning myself, but I was just thanking the good Lord that my little children in there can have their larning."

According to the last census, of the 4,600,000 colored people of ten years old and upward, 1,400,000 (or about 30 per cent.) have learned to read and write. There have been two colored men in the United States Senate, and several in the different departments of government, and many in the legislatures of all the States. Frederick Douglass, who once escaped from the hands of the United States marshal of the District of Columbia, has since been the United States marshal in the same District.

In every way we have reason to be thankful for the great progress made throughout the whole Southern country both by the whites and the colored people.

Although slavery was virtually destroyed by the proclamation of Lincoln, it was legally ended only when the following amendments became part of the Constitution of the United States.

The thirteenth amendment is as follows :—

ARTICLE XIV.—*Section* 1.—Neither slavery nor involuntary servitude, except as a punishment for crime, whereof the party shall have been duly convicted, shall exist within the United States, or any place subject to their jurisdiction.

The fourteenth amendment defines who are citizens, to be equally protected in all the States.

The fifteenth amendment is this :—

ARTICLE XV.—*Section* 1.—The right of citizens of the United States to vote shall not be denied or abridged by the United States, or by any State, on account of race, color, or previous condition of servitude.

The proclamation of Lincoln was the corner-stone ; these amendments to the Constitution were the key-stone of the arch of Liberty.

In view of these great results of the struggle I have thus briefly described, we can well adopt the language of Lowell's commemoration poem, the finest English ode, perhaps, since Wordsworth's Ode to Immortality, to express a nation's joy in the coming of universal freedom, and the creation of a better union in our land.